THESMART PLAYBOOK™

Game-changing life skills for a modern world

To Dylan, Gavin & Liam,
Always "Play it SMART!"
Best, Syzan Wind

Suzanne M. Wind

First Printing 2014

ISBN: 13 978-1495211621
ISBN: 10 1495211622

ModernGrace Publishing
Greenwich, CT

thesmartplaybook@gmail.com
www.thesmartplaybook.com

Order Information: Special discounts are available on quantity purchase by corporation, associations, educators and others. For details contact the publisher at the above email address.

SMART

PRAISE AND AWARDS

The Mom's Choice Awards® among the best in family-friendly media, products and services at the highest - gold - level.

Honored with the distinguished *Creative Child Magazine 2014 Book of the Year* Award, one of today's foremost children's education publications.

Multiple Awards from **The Toy Man®** *News and Reviews* - a highly recognized international leader in independent product and service evaluation:

The Toy Man® "Award of Excellence"
The Toy Man® S.T.E.M Award
The Toy Man® eChoice Award
The Toy Man® "Mom-Approved - Comme Il Faut" Award

Proud Recipient of 7 Prestigious Awards!

Recognized with the **Mr. Dad Seal of Approval,** an endorsement that carries the powerful credibility of Americans leading authority on successful fatherhood.

"I TRULY love the whole concept. Parents can make sure their children develop vital social skills while having a fun experience with kids. The information is helpful and the tone is pitch-perfect."
> - **Dr. Andrea Archibald,** *Child Psychologist and Chief Girl Expert for Girls Scouts of USA*

"As we all know, most of the very important life lessons are learned at home. This workbook is a great 'family project' to help teach and reinforce vital life skills - fun and social skill building all-in-one."
> - **Anita Kulick,** *President & CEO, Educating Communities for Parenting*

"...this is where the fantastic book **The SMART Playbook** by **Suzanne M Wind** comes into play, quite literally This book's curriculum teaches your child or students real life manners and practical skills in a very relatable and child friendly format."
> - **Jill R.** @ *Enchanted Homeschooling Mom*

"...a practical guide to building social skills in a fun and engaging format. A great tool to help children and their families."
> - **Dr. Karen Beckman,** *Riverside Pediatrics*

DEDICATION & ACKNOWLEDGEMENTS:

This book is dedicated to my family. To my mormor and morfar, the two most socially graceful people I've ever known. To my mom and dad who raised me with an appreciation for manners—always reminding me to respect life's little unwritten rules. Thank you to my sons Charlie & Nicky, whom I credit for the sports theme and the stick figures. And to my little Annie who inspired the crown to top it off. Finally, I love you Chad—thanks for believing in The SMART Playbook every day.

CONTENTS

⇨ A WORD TO THE COACHES (That Means You, Parents!)

The SMART Playbook was founded by a mom of three, with a possibly impossible mission: to offer families a simple and effective game plan to teach relevant life skills for a modern world. Teaching social skills and manners in this fast-paced, tech-focused society is easier said than done. How do we get our kids back to basics without overwhelming our time?

THE SOLUTION: The SMART Playbook. Written in a relatable style and chock full of games, The SMART Playbook will lead you and your child in a collaborative effort to bring manners to a new generation. Your child is the player, the book is the guide, and you are the coach. Life is the referee.

5 SMART topics to help your child succeed in life:
  + Social Skill Basics – The principles of modern manners
  + Mealtime Manners – A guide to mealtime etiquette
  + Art of Conversation – Eloquent face-to-face conversational skills
  + Restaurant Behavior – The finer points of restaurant conduct
  + Technology Talk – Internet safety and responsible usage

THE BENEFIT: The methods included in The SMART Playbook will help your child gain confidence, character, integrity and empathy in face-to-face situations and technology usage.

HOW TO USE: Fill out the SMART contract. (This will help motivate your child to complete the lessons.) As your child completes game challenges, he or she earns tickets and you decide the prizes. As the coach, your job is to encourage your child to work on the lessons and take the challenges. When you play the family scrimmage games, reward your child with lots of tickets!

THE RESULT: A happy and confident child thriving in a modern world.

⇨ PLAYER INTRODUCTION

Dear Player,

Getting older is awesome, but there's also more expected
of you. If you know the guidelines for interacting with
people, growing up is so much easier.

Social skills and manners are the keys to having great friends, gaining
respect from adults and growing your self-confidence. Wouldn't it
be great to know the ins and outs of all the rules to guide you?

The SMART Playbook lets you in on commonsense guidelines.
Through games and challenges you will learn how to handle all sorts
of new situations both in person and while using technology. And to
top it off, you will look like a star player!

Have a great time playing, and best of luck!

From,
Suzanne Wind, the author of The SMART Playbook

GAME ON!

Ready to get in the game yet?
Accept the challenge? Fill out the SMART Contract on the next
page. Then move on to earn tickets and win prizes. **Ready, Set, Go!**

THE SMART CONTRACT

This is an agreement between you and your parents. Here's your chance to ask for a cool prize in exchange for learning game-changing life skills. It's a win-win situation.

What's a win-win situation, you might ask? It means you earn something super-cool (and of your own choosing!) by simply learning life rules and plays. **Please fill this out before you begin.**

Date: _____

I _____ agree to carefully read and complete The SMART Playbook.

1) I promise to share one fact every time I learn something new with the rest of the family.

2) I promise to share many games and activities so that my family can practice modern manners together.

3) Each time I finish a game challenge I'll earn a ticket. My parents promise to reward me with the following (Make sure to determine how many tickets you need to win!):

_____

_____

_____

_____

4) After completing this entire playbook, (besides being a Star Player) my parents agree to reward me with the following:

_____

_____

_____

_____

Good Luck Playing!

_____   _____
Player Signature   Coach Signature

⇨ **LET THE GAMES BEGIN!**

THE GOAL:

Learn and use modern manners and social skills to help you get along with all people and make you feel more confident. Think of it this way: there are set rules in sports to ensure fair play and to give everyone an equal chance to win. Practice and dedication makes you a great athlete.

Practice and dedication helps you learn SMART plays and wins you the Golden ticket to being your best in life.

Life Skills Required:
The playbook is divided into five SMART game sections: Social Skill Basics, Mealtime Manners, Art of Conversation, Restaurant Behavior and Technology Talk.

Equipment Needed:

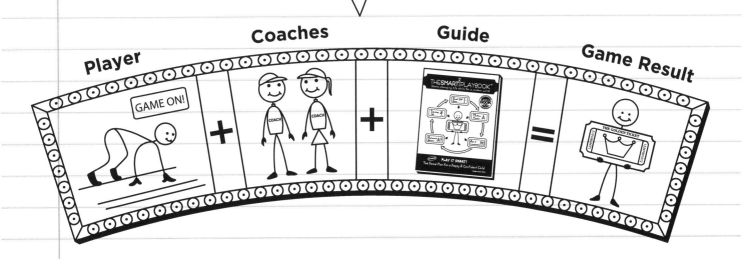

How to play to WIN

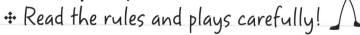

- ✤ Read the rules and plays carefully!
- ✤ Pay attention to the RULE BREAKERS!
- ✤ Learn and earn the **game tickets**. How many can you win? Each game challenge is worth one ticket. Play the game challenge more than once and earn additional tickets.
- ✤ Study the WINNING PLAY REVIEWS.
- ✤ **Game On** - Practice!

GAME ON!

Life is your referee. The more tickets you learn and earn the bigger the reward. Fill out the Ticket Tally Score Board after each game. Have Fun!

GAME PLAN #1 — SOCIAL SKILLS BASICS

GOAL:

Basic social skills teach you everyday rules that make life easier. Learn how to make good choices and how to act politely in different situations.

Life Skills Required:

- ❖ First Impressions 101
- ❖ Telephone Smarts
- ❖ Host & Guest Rules
- ❖ Commitment
- ❖ Good Sportsmanship

Equipment needed:

- ❖ You
- ❖ Parents, siblings and friends to play the games

Game Directions:

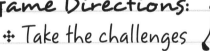

- ❖ Take the challenges
- ❖ Have an adult check the box at the end of the game after you complete the challenge
- ❖ Cash in your tickets for the reward chosen with your coach (your parents)

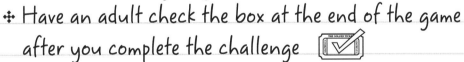

Ticket Goal:_____

Game Prize:_____

FiRST iMPRESSiONS

A first impression is what a person thinks of you the first time he meets you. This might be the first time you go to your new friend's house and meet her family or the first day of school when you meet your teacher. Making a good impression depends on your appearance, the way you present yourself and the way you communicate. You only get one chance to make a great first impression so make it BIG!

> HANDLE YOURSELF WITH GOOD MANNERS AND YOU WILL LEAVE A GOOD IMPRESSION

RULE BREAKER!

✣ **DON'T:** A little boy goes on his first playdate. He charges inside the house and does not say hello. The first thing out of his mouth is "I MUST DESTROY!" He stays for dinner, burps at the table and screams for seconds. What type of first impression did he leave at this house? Do you think the parents were eager to have him come back and play? Probably not, right?

GAME CHALLENGE #1: Can you think of 5 great plays to make a good first impression?

1.

2.

3.

4

5.

Be Courteous & Respectful

What does it mean to be courteous and respectful? Courteous is a word used to describe someone who is polite, respectful and considerate. It shows people that you are concerned about others. It makes people feel that you value them when you have good manners. And it shows that you have integrity. Integrity is a personal characteristic that says, "I am honest, and have high standards." The best way to remind yourself to be courteous and respectful is to follow THE GOLDEN RULE! The Golden Rule is, "Do unto others, as you would have them do unto you." Make wise choices and be courteous and respectful to all.

THE GOLDEN RULE: DO UNTO OTHERS, AS YOU WOULD HAVE THEM DO UNTO YOU.

Top RESPECTFUL "After you" Plays:

❖ **Hold doors open.** If you are going through a door with a friend, let her go ahead of you and say, "After you, please." Hold a door open for an older person or someone who is carrying a lot of stuff.

❖ **Let them talk.** If you are having a conversation with someone and you both start talking at the same time, let your friend go first. "After you, please."

❖ **Your guest goes first.** Even if you are really thirsty, pour your friend's drink first. And when there's just one cookie left, offer it to your friend.

❖ **Offer your seat to a stranger.** If you are on a crowded bus or train, give up your seat to anybody who looks as if he needs it. Older people and pregnant women are always great candidates for this!

GAME CHALLENGE #2: Do you follow the Golden Rule? Here's your chance to make good choices. Circle the wise choice.

1. Your mom tells you to clean your room. You:
    a. Pay your little sister to clean it.
    b. Clean it.
    c. Promise to clean it after school.

2. You see some kids take another kid's ball and run away. You:
    a. Don't do anything.
    b. Run after the kids and try to help him get it back.
    c. Tell the kid he needs to stand up for himself.

Be Tactful

Having tact is the ability to deal with others without offending them. It is the ability to be honest but to use words that don't hurt the other person's feelings. See the positive instead of focusing on the negative. By emphasizing the positive you can provide tactfully honest answers that do not upset anyone. Look at the other person's body language and facial expressions to know if you are making them sad or uncomfortable. Can you deal with a situation honestly, but considerately?

> **HAVE TACT! SEE THE POSITIVE INSTEAD OF FOCUSING ON THE NEGATIVE.**

GAME CHALLENGE #3: TACTFUL PLAYS

SITUATION	YOUR HONEST THOUGHT?	RUDE RESPONSE	TACTFUL RESPONSE
Your mom just cooked a new recipe. She worked for hours putting together the dish.	That looks really gross and I don't think I can eat It.	Uhh. Gross!	Thanks, Mom, for cooking a special meal. I really appreciate it.
For your birthday, your aunt gives you a sweater which you think is ugly. When she asks if you like it, what should you say?			
Your friend is talking and has a giant piece of green lettuce stuck between his teeth. What should you say?			

RULE BREAKER!

✤ DON'T blurt out the first thing that pops in your head. Find ways to express thoughts where no one is hurt.

✤ DON'T ignore other people's feelings. Be sensitive to body language and facial expressions to know when to stop.

GAME CHALLENGE #4: Do you have tact? Challenge your family or friends to draw a self-portrait in five minutes. Then everyone has to give one nice compliment about the drawing.

Posture & Confidence

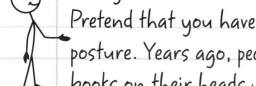

Walk the Walk!

Always stand tall and walk with confidence.
Pretend that you have something holding you up to give you great posture. Years ago, people used to practice good posture by balancing books on their heads while walking.

GAME CHALLENGE #5: WHO LOOKS MORE CONFIDENT?

Circle the right answer!

Get Up and Stand Tall

The most polite way to greet someone is to first stand up. So what if you are in the middle of your video game or watching a really cool show? You should still stand up out of respect, thoughtfulness or consideration. Then say hello!

Now sometimes, the person might say, "Oh please don't stand up" and then you can sit back down. But your first instinct should always be to stop what you are doing, stand up and say hello.

 GAME CHALLENGE #6: The Great Balancing Act. Walk across the room balancing a book on your head. Stand up straight with your head held high and shoulders back. Challenge your siblings to see who can walk the farthest and straightest.

Always Say Hello

Have you ever, said **"Hello"** to someone and then instead
of them saying "Hi" back they either looked down or
away? How does that make you feel? It can hurt your
feelings, right? Silence might mean "I'm mad at you" or "I don't really like you."

Hello in different languages
Danish – "Hey!"
Swedish – "Hej!"
French – "Bonjour"
Italian – "Ciao!"
Spanish – "Hola"
German – "Hallo"
Hawaiian – "Aloha"
Japanese – "Konnichiwa"

> ACKNOWLEDGE THE
> PRESENCE OF ANOTHER
> PERSON!

So even if you are feeling sad, angry, busy, late, afraid, or
embarrassed always say hello. We say hello to let the other
person know that we have noticed him or her.

RULE BREAKERS!

✤ DON'T look away and pretend that you don't know someone.

Make Eye Contact 👀

> EYE CONTACT SHOWS
> RESPECT, INTEREST, CARE,
> AND THAT YOU APPRECIATE
> WHAT IS BEING SAID!

Always look people in the eye when saying hello (even
if you feel a little shy). Eye contact shows that you are
friendly and honest. It shows that you care and have an interest in them. Not
looking someone in the eye can make you look suspicious and untrustworthy.

GAME CHALLENGE #7: Tell a friend everything you did from the
moment you woke up until this very moment. While you are
talking, your friend should never take his eyes off your
face-he should stare at you. How do you feel?

Now try this same activity two other ways.
✤ Your friend should never look at your face. How do you feel?
✤ Your friend should look at your face some of the time. How do
you feel?

Use Names

Always greet people by their name. What is the difference between "Hi" and "Hi, Mr. Smith"? By using a name, it shows that you care who they are, which makes people feel good. Sometimes it's hard to remember other people's names. Here's a little tip: When you first meet someone say their name three times to yourself.

> GREET PEOPLE BY THEIR NAME TO SHOW YOU CARE!

"Her name is Annie, Annie, and Annie." Then use it in a sentence out loud before you leave. "It is so nice to meet you, Annie."

Shake Hands

> STAND TALL AND CONFIDENT. TAKE A STEP FORWARD AND REACH OUT YOUR HAND. GIVE A FIRM SHAKE!

Step up and shake hands when you are saying hello to an adult, especially in a formal setting. Stand tall and straight. Hold your head up and pull your shoulders in. Take a confident step forward, reach out your right hand and say the person's name: "Hi, Mrs. Jones." Clasp the person's hand firmly and give it a small, quick shake. Do not use what we call a "jello" or "spaghetti" handshake. Your handshake should be firm and not squirmy and light. Use your full hand; don't just use your fingers. And don't over-shake. One or two shakes is plenty.

RULE BREAKER!

* DON'T look down or at the TV while talking to someone.
* DON'T pretend that you don't know someone.
* DON'T use a "jello" hand to greet someone.

GAME CHALLENGE #8: The Perfect Handshake. Shake someone's hand today. Stand up tall, speak clearly and use their name. Don't forget eye contact. Give it a quick firm shake.

Titles & Forms of Address

Countries and cultures have different customs of how to address someone. In the U.S., there's a set of basic title rules. A modern version allows you to call people by what they like to be called. So if an adult invites you to call them by their first name, then go ahead. If you are not sure what to call someone, always use the more formal approach. (See chart)

KNOW THE 'BASIC TITLE RULES'. ASK HOW SOMEONE WOULD LIKE TO BE ADDRESSED.

BASIC TITLE RULES:

Mr.	=	a man
Mrs.	=	a married woman
Ms.	=	a woman, married or unmarried
Mr. & Ms.	=	a couple with different last names
Mr. & Mrs.	=	a couple with the same last name
Miss	=	a girl or unmarried woman

There are also a lot of special rules that apply to special people like doctors, university professors, diplomats, religious leaders and more. Most likely you will be told what to call them, but when in doubt ask a grown up.

GAME CHALLENGE #9: Fill in the blank.

Your teacher's name is Sarah Smith. She is married. Hi, _____ Smith.

Your dad's friend's name is John James. Hi, _____ James.

Your doctor's name is Joyce Jones. She is married. Hi, _____ Jones.

Your mom's friend is Jane John. She has asked you to call her Jane. Hi, _____.

TELEPHONE SMARTS

Who's afraid of the big bad telephone? Talking on the phone is different than meeting someone in person or writing them a text or email. There's no face-to-face to help understand what the other person is thinking or doing. For example, the person on the other end can't just give a nod to show you that he is ready to end the call. Master and apply simple telephone skills to make you more comfortable.

> **APPLY BASIC PHONE RULES TO SOUND CONFIDENT!**

Answering a Phone

> **ANSWER THE PHONE WITH A PROPER GREETING AND POLITELY HAND OVER THE PHONE. TAKE GOOD MESSAGES!**

Don't be afraid-just pick up the phone! There are several ways to answer. Some people use a simple "Hello" or you might prefer something more formal like "Hello, The Eveland residence". If the call is for your mom, say, "Sure, one moment please. May I ask who is calling?" Then carry the phone to your mom, cover the receiver, and quietly identify the caller to your mom. **Please don't shout at the top of your lungs, "PHONE FOR YOU!!! AMY IS ON THE PHONE FOR YOU!!!"** If they ask for your brother and he is not home or he is busy, say, "I'm sorry Charlie is not home right now. Would you like me to take a message?" Write the message down clearly and leave it somewhere safe. You can also ask the caller if he/she prefers to call back and leave a message on the machine. Then let the phone ring until the voicemail picks up.

If a friend calls when you are having dinner, you can just let him or her know that you are in the middle of dinner and that you'll call them back in a while.

> Hello. Sure, one moment please. May I ask who is calling?

GAME CHALLENGE #10: Q&A

1. What if your mom is in the shower when someone calls?
2. What do you do if you call the wrong number by mistake?

Making a Call

Hi. This is Nicky. May I please speak with Charlie? Thank you.

Always identify yourself when making a call. Even if it sounds like your friend picking up, you should still say your name. Then make sure you respond to the person answering the phone with a "thank you."

> ALWAYS IDENTIFY YOURSELF AND CALL DURING APPROPRIATE TIMES.

Remember to call at appropriate times. Call after 9 am in the morning, especially on the weekend. Avoid calling during dinner hours.

Talking on the Phone

> PAY 100% ATTENTION TO THE PHONE CALL. SPEAKING CLEARLY!

Give your full attention to the person you are speaking to. Do not try to multi-task-watching TV, reading a book, playing video games-while trying to speak. And do not stuff food in your mouth, please! The phone should be held with one end up to your ear and the other end (receiver) up to your mouth. Speak clearly and loudly.

Ending a Call

> SAY A PROPER GOODBYE TO END A CALL.

End a phone call politely. For example, you might say, "I should probably get started on my homework" or "It was really nice talking to you. See you tomorrow." If you just say "Bye" you end the phone call very abruptly which isn't nice. Keep in mind that the other person can't see your facial expressions. He doesn't see the smile or nod that shows that you are about to hang up.

> **GAME CHALLENGE #11:** Pick up the big bad telephone! Call someone -your cousin, your grandmother, a friend... Remember to identify yourself.

RULE BREAKERS!

✢ DON'T answer the phone with 'uh-huh.'

✢ DON'T call someone without introducing yourself.

✢ DON'T eat while talking on the phone.

✢ DON'T hang up without saying goodbye properly.

✢ DON'T use the following words: 'yeah,' 'yup,' 'who's this?', 'what do you want?', 'why are you calling?'

GAME CHALLENGE #12: Create your telephone Cheat Sheet.

TELEPHONE REMINDERS

Calling: Hi, this is _____. May I please speak to _____.

Answering: Hi, the Smiths.

Responding: Just a minute please. I'll go get my mom.

Message: I am sorry, my dad can't come to the phone right now. May, I please take a message?

Call waiting: I am sorry, that's my other line, could you hold on for a minute. Thank you.

Wrong #:   I'm sorry. I must have dialed the wrong number.

Ending Call: Thank you for calling.

TELEPHONE REMINDERS - Fill in the blanks.

Calling: Hi, this is

Answering:

Responding:

Message:

Call waiting:

Wrong #:

Ending Call:

HOST OR GUEST BASICS

The best way to have fun at playdates and parties is to learn how to be a good host or guest. The most important rule is to always make everyone feel welcome and comfortable. And if you are going to someone's house or to a party, follow their house rules and don't break their stuff!

You're in Charge

Top HOST Plays:

Hello - Say hello to your friends at the door. Show them where to put their shoes or coats. If they have never met your family, introduce them and show them around.

Share the Rules - Let them know any special house or party rules. Maybe a parent works from home and you cannot go play in the downstairs office. Or perhaps you are not allowed to play with toys that belong to your brother or sister. Is the dog friendly? Is your brother's room off-limits?

Be Flexible - Try to be flexible on what to do. Come up with different activities and ask your friend what he would like to do.

Welcome - Make your friend feel welcome. Ask them if they would like a drink or something to eat.

A HOST MAKES PEOPLE FEEL WELCOME AND COMFORTABLE!

Goodbye - Always follow your guest to the door to say goodbye (even if you would rather finish playing the rest of the video game or watching a little more of the TV show...) And make sure you thank them for coming over!

GAME CHALLENGE #13: Play Host. Invite a friend over and make him feel welcome in your home. Name three things you could do to make him feel comfortable?

1._____ 2._____ 3._____

Follow the Leader

TIME OUT!

Q: Why are owls always invited to the party?
A: Because they are such a hoot!

Top GUEST Plays:

Hello - Say hello to everyone in the house. Take your shoes and coat off and ask where you should put them. Don't just throw your stuff in a big pile in the hallway!

Learn and Follow rules - Make sure to do what your host asks. If your friend tells you that you cannot disturb his older brother, listen. Never wander around a house by yourself. Stick with your friend and let him guide you. Respect all the belongings of the house. Don't jump on their couch or climb on furniture.

> A GUEST SHOULD BE RESPECTFUL AND FOLLOW THE RULES!

Goodbye - Thank your friend for inviting you over to his house or to a party. It is also nice to thank the parents. Thanking them all will leave a really good impression!

Gifts

How do you accept a gift gracefully? The first thing is to always say something positive about each gift. "What a cool toy." "This is just what I wanted." Never ask how much something cost. And if someone didn't bring a present never embarrass them by asking where it is. You can always make something if you don't have the money to buy something. Handmade gifts are nice and personable! What do you do if you already have something or if you don't like the gift? Regardless of how you feel you should always say something positive about the present.

> ALWAYS SAY SOMETHING POSITIVE WHEN YOU RECEIVE A GIFT.

RULE BREAKERS!

- ❖ DON'T ask someone how much something cost.
- ❖ DON'T put the gift aside and not say anything.

Thank You Notes

A little note can make such a difference! The purpose of a thank you note is to let a person know how much his or her generosity and kindness are appreciated. It doesn't have to be long - a brief thoughtful note is all that you need.

The Steps
Begin by talking about the gift. Say something positive. Have you used it? Did someone else comment on it? What did you really like about it?
Then you thank them for coming to your party or house.
To end the note, just thank them a second time.

When should you write a thank you? The general rule is that if you open a gift when the giver is there and thank him in person sending a note is not necessary. (Now that doesn't mean that you can't write a thank you note anytime. Why not write a quick thank you to let them know how much you are enjoying the gift!) But if you receive a present by mail or open presents later, it is important to write a thank you note.

TAKE THE TIME TO WRITE A THOUGHTFUL THANK YOU NOTE.

Always try to write something specific about the gift. If you get a gift certificate or money tell them what you plan to do with it.

Begin by either making your own card or buying ready-made cards. In today's modern world, it's even acceptable to write a nice email. (Don't just type a few lines but give it a little more thought and maybe attach a picture of you playing with your new toy.) A hand-written note is an even nicer touch! It shows that you took a little extra time.

Dear Joe,

Thank you so much for the cool baseball shirt. I love playing baseball and will definitely use this shirt all the time.

It was really fun having you at my party! ☺

Thanks again for the cool shirt.

Your friend,
Charlie

TIME OUT!

Q: Which hand is better to write with?

A: Neither, it's best to write with a pen!

GAME CHALLENGE #14: Send a thank you note to someone - your coach, your teacher, a friend, a family member......

COMMITMENT

Commitment means doing what needs to be done regardless of your talents or your mood. Even if you are sad, mad, tired or if something better comes along you still need to follow through on a commitment. All activities--academic, athletic and social--should be followed through with a positive attitude and determination.

For example, you have committed to work with your math partner to complete a homework project but then your best friend invites you to the park to play.

> COMMITMENT IS A PROMISE THAT YOU MUST FOLLOW THROUGH.

Although the park sounds like more fun, you still need to keep your commitment to work with your math partner. Breaking one social commitment for another can hurt someone's feelings and is just bad manners. The same applies to athletics: If you're on a sports team, and you don't show up for an important game, you let your whole team down.

TOP COMMITMENT Plays:

- ✤ Have an "I-can-do-it" attitude.
- ✤ I will try my hardest.
- ✤ I will keep working until I reach my goal.
- ✤ If at first you don't succeed, try again.
- ✤ Quitters never win.
- ✤ Winners never quit.
- ✤ Finish what you started.

GAME CHALLENGE #15:

How have you ever given up? What could you have done different?

Make a family commitment slogan. Use any of the 'top commitment plays' or make a new one.

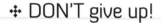

RULE BREAKERS!

✤ DON'T break commitments!

✤ DON'T over-commit. Try to stay balanced and don't commit to too many activities and events.

✤ DON'T give up!

GOOD SPORTSMANSHIP

"It's not whether you win or lose, it's how you play the game." - Anonymous Always play fair and be polite. Good sportsmanship is when teammates, opponents, coaches, and officials treat each other with respect.

Character

PRACTICING GOOD SPORTSMANSHIP MAKES YOU A GREAT ATHLETE!

You can tell a lot about someone's character by how they play sports. Character is made up of our values and our decisions. It is who we are when no one is looking. It is a trait that can help you in all parts of your life-not just sports. No matter what the score is at the end of the game, if you play with character, you win!

Top SPORTSMANSHIP Plays:

1. Follow and obey the game rules.
2. Support your teammates.
3. Respect your coach and the referees.
4. Try your hardest.
5. Play to have fun.
6. Cheer for good play (your team or your opponents).
7. Shake hands after the game.

HAVING CHARACTER MEANS DOING THE RIGHT THING BECAUSE IT IS THE RIGHT THING TO DO.

And if you happen to sit out of a game, remember good sportsmanship extends to the sidelines. If you are watching, never cheer if the opponent makes a mistake. Never be tempted to shout out rude comments about your team's opponents or boo them! Never try to distract a player by sneezing or shouting out something as he/she is trying to concentrate.

25

RULE BREAKERS!

- ✤ DON'T trip someone or call your opponent by names to discourage or distract them.
- ✤ DON'T show up inappropriately dressed or unprepared for practice.
- ✤ DON'T cheat or argue with the referee.
- ✤ DON'T refuse to shake hands when you lose.
- ✤ DON'T brag if you win or be a poor sport if you lose.

GAME CHALLENGE #16: Name 3 things you could do to show good character and great sportsmanship:

1.

2.

3.

SMART

WINNING PLAY REVIEW

Game Plan #1 - Social Skill Basics

1. Handle yourself with good manners and you will leave a good impression.
2. The Golden Rule: "Do unto others as you would have them do unto you."
3. Have tact! See the positive instead of focusing on the negative.
4. Stand up tall and straight to look confident.
5. Stand up to greet someone new and important.
6. Acknowledge the presence of another person.
7. Make eye contact to show respect, interest, care and that you appreciate what is being said.
8. Greet people by their name to show you care.
9. When shaking hands, take a step forward and reach out your hand. Give a firm shake.
10. Change the greeting based on who and when you are meeting someone.
11. Know the 'basic title rules'. Ask how someone would like to be addressed.
12. Apply basic phone rules to sound confident.
13. Answer the phone with a proper greeting and politely hand over the phone. Take good messages.
14. Identify yourself and call during appropriate times.
15. Pay 100% attention to the phone call, speaking clearly.
16. Say a proper goodbye to end a call.
17. A host makes people feel welcome and comfortable in your home.
18. A guest should be respectful and follow the rules.
19. Say something positive when you receive a gift.
20. Take the time to write a thoughtful thank you note
21. Commitment is a promise that you must follow through.
22. Practicing good sportsmanship makes you a great athlete.
23. Having character means doing the right thing because it is the right thing to do.

LET'S PRACTICE!

GAME ON!

SECTION 1. You make the call!

Fill in the blanks with **DO** or **DON'T**. Complete this section and earn 10 tickets!

1. _____Your friend just tripped in front of a bunch of other kids. You laugh at her—after all, she just tripped.

2. _____You go to a special event without your brother and they are giving out free cookies. You say thank you and ask if you could possibly get one more for your brother who is home sick. You showed concern for your brother and wanted to try to make him feel better.

3. _____You go to shake Mrs. Anderson's hand and she uses a soft flimsy handshake. You still shake her hand firmly and stand up tall.

4. _____You are on a crowded bus and are sitting comfortably. An elderly person walks onto the bus. Think to yourself, "Wow I am lucky that I have a seat. That's too bad that she has to stand".

5. _____Your mom walks in with her hands full of grocery bags while you are playing video games. Ignore her and continue to play the video game. After all, it's a very cool game.

6. _____The competition is about to take a penalty shot. To distract the player you begin to sneeze loudly and make disturbing noises.

7. _____You just got a present from your Aunt Peggy. You have the same sweater at home. You don't let her know and thank her so much for the lovely sweater.

8. _____You go to John's house to play. When he's not looking you sneak a couple of cookies from the pantry. His mom said to help yourself—might as well stuff a couple of cookies in your mouth!

9. _____You rush to go through the door but slow down when you realize someone is behind you. You decide to hold the door open and let them go first.

SECTION 2. Scrimmage!

Some of these games you can play on your own. For others, recruit family and friends to play with you! Each game is worth one ticket. The more times you play, the more you earn.

What's Your Name? Learn someone's name today. Try repeating a new friend's name three times to yourself so that you won't forget their name. Say the name out loud in a sentence. "It's really nice to see you again, Sam".

The Perfect Handshake! Shake someone's hand today. Remember a firm and quick shake. Stand up tall, speak clearly and use their name. And don't forget to make eye contact.

Do You have Tact? Go around the room and give one nice compliment about the outfit of the person next to you. (Even if you don't like the clothes, find something positive to say.)

Great Stare-Down Challenge Practice looking into someone's eyes while speaking. Grab a partner and tell them a two-minute story while looking the person straight in the eye. Here's where you can have a little fun. Who can tell the funniest story and make the other person look away from laughing?

You Make the Call! What are the right answers? Discuss your answers with your parents.

  ✤ You've just taken a bite out of a big sandwich and the phone rings. Should you answer it or let the machine pick up?
  ✤ You answer the phone and a company is offering a magazine subscrip tion. What do you do?

❖ You are on the phone with your friend and the other line is ringing? What do you do?

❖ You answer the phone and it is a call for your mom. She's in the shower? What do you do?

❖ You are talking to your grandmother but you really are running out of things to say. What should you do?

❖ You call your friend to ask about a homework assignment. He doesn't seem to be home and the machine picks up. What should you do?

❖ Your mom is on the phone. Should you and your brother start singing and dancing loudly in front of her?

❖ A stranger calls your house and asks for someone you don't know. What should you do?

NOTE: Never give a stranger any personal information!

SECTION 3. Social Skills Word Search - Earn 5 tickets! ☺

```
Q L G Z H J S A L O T V Z Y N
T F Z O P A B K L Z A A P T S
E T C E I C N L N R W O C L P
L Y F I H H E D A A S U L T F
E G B Y S H R R S T H I R R U
P S U U N H U U U H K T K W Z
H X B B A D I R E S A E L P P
O I Z F M U E L L W H K W V H
N K I V S C S A J G S T E Q W
E F M K T K I G S W W S Q M G
V V A M R C O N F I D E N C E
S N E S O P P B U A L U K M E
O L L S P H K Q W F K G L A J
L F H V S F P L H O S T V E Y
W H R D O S E P V L V M Q V M
```

CONFIDENCE   GUEST
HANDSHAKE   HELLO
HOST   PLEASE
POSTURE   SOCIAL SKILLS
SPORTSMANSHIP   TACT
TELEPHONE   THANKS

SECTION 4. Social Skills Crossword Puzzle

- Earn 5 tickets! ☺

Across ▷

2. A promise that you need to follow through with.

7. A word used to describe someone polite, respectful and considerate.

8. A personal characteristic that says, "I am honest and I have high standards."

Down

1. It is who we are when no one is looking.

3. The ability to deal with others without offending them.

4. How we stand.

5. Your job is to be respectful and follow the rules.

6. Your job is to make people feel welcome and comfortable.

Words to Play: Courteous, Integrity, Tact, Commitment, Character, Posture, Host and Guest.

ANSWERS

Game Challenges:

#1) Answers will vary. Please discuss with your coach (an adult).

#2) 1. b - Clean it.

2. b - Run after the kids and try to help him get it back.

#3) Answers will vary. Please discuss with your coach (an adult).

#4) Answers will vary. Please discuss with your coach (an adult).

#5) Stick figure with glasses.

#6) Remember to balance the books and walk as straight as you can - good luck!

#7) Answers will vary. Please discuss with your coach (an adult).

#8) Firm hand shake, please.

#9) Hi, Ms. Smith. Hi, Mr. James. Hi, Dr. Jones. Hi, Jane.

#10) 1. Please let the caller know that your mom cannot come to the phone right now and ask if you could take a message.

2. I'm sorry I think I dialed the wrong number. Is this 203-555-1557? Please don't just hang up; that would be rude. Then recheck the number before dialing again.

#11) Hi, this is _____. May I please speak with _____.

#12) Tip: Keep your cheat sheet by the phone.

#13) Answers will vary. Please discuss with your coach (an adult).

#14) Use the 'Thank You Guide' in the back to help write your note.

#15) Answers will vary. Please discuss with your coach (an adult).

#16) Answers will vary. Please discuss with your coach (an adult).

Game On

SECTION 1. You make the call!

1. Don't, 2. Do, 3. Do, 4. Don't, 5. Don't, 6. Don't, 7. Do, 8. Don't, 9. Do

SECTION 2. Scrimmage!

Answers will vary. Please discuss answers with your coach (an adult).

SECTION 3. Word Search

```
+  +  +  +  H  +  S  +  +  O  T  +  +  +  +
T  +  +  +  P  A  +  K  L  +  +  A  P  +  S
E  +  +  +  I  +  N  L  N  +  +  O  C  L  +
L  +  +  +  H  +  E  D  +  A  S  +  L  T  +
E  +  +  +  S  H  +  +  S  T  H  I  +  +  +
P  +  +  +  N  +  +  +  U  H  K  T  +  +  +
H  +  +  +  A  +  +  R  E  S  A  E  L  P  +
O  +  +  +  M  +  E  +  L  +  +  K  +  +  +
N  +  +  +  S  +  +  A  +  +  +  T  E  +  +
E  +  +  +  T  +  I  +  +  +  +  S  +  +  +
+  +  +  +  R  C  O  N  F  I  D  E  N  C  E
+  +  +  +  O  +  +  +  +  +  +  U  +  +  +
+  +  +  S  P  +  +  +  +  +  +  G  +  +  +
+  +  +  +  S  +  +  +  H  O  S  T  +  +  +
+  +  +  +  +  +  +  +  +  +  +  +  +  +  +
```

(Over, Down, Direction)

CONFIDENCE(6,11,E)

GUEST(12,13,N)

HANDSHAKE(5,1,SE)

HELLO(6,5,NE)

HOST(9,14,E)

PLEASE(14,7,W)

POSTURE(13,2,SW)

SOCIALSKILLS(4,13,NE)

SPORTSMANSHIP(5,14,N)

TACT(11,1,SE)

TELEPHONE(1,2,S)

THANKS(12,6,NW)

SECTION 4. Crossword Puzzle

Across ⇨   2. Commitment   7. Courteous   8. Integrity

Down ⇩   1. Character   3. Tact   4. Posture   5. Guest   6. Host

34

TICKET TALLY SCORE BOARD

Ask an adult to place a check on a ticket after each game challenge or practice section. How many tickets were you able to collect?

SCORE BOARD
X · X · X

SMART

THANK YOU DRILL

Follow the guide and add your creative play! Fill in the name and replace the number with words. Use the list or come up with something original!

#1

awesome gift

cool present

perfect gift

thoughtful gift

fun gift

yummy cake

_____(name of the gift)

_____(be creative!)

#2

play with it

use it

try it

test it out

eat it

_____(something original)

#3

Mention the gift again. Here you can choose something from list #1 again.

Dear _____ Name _____.

Thank you so much for the _____ 1 _____.

I love it! I can't wait to _____ 2 _____.
That was very kind of you to remember me.

Thanks again for _____ 3 _____.

Hope to see you soon.

Sincerely,

_____

2-POINT CONVERSION TO TOP IT OFF:

Score bonus points and add a little extra to your card....

‡ A photo of you playing with your new toy
‡ Bake something to bring with your card
‡ A drawing

A MORE CREATIVE PLAY:

A techy modern thank you!

Use the smartphone to create a unique thank you with your own words and personality.

‡ Create a picture with captions
‡ A video that captures your excitement opening the gift and how grateful you are!
‡ Send a picture by email or text of you wearing the new coat holding up a thank you sign
‡ Create a video of yourself playing soccer with the new ball

GAME PLAN #2 - MEALTIME MANNERS

GOAL:

Have you ever seen pigs eat at the farm? The farmer pours the food down and the pigs all swarm the food in a feeding frenzy. They will grab, push, snort and gulp down as much food as possible.

You might be in a hurry to get to a game or super hungry after a long day at school, but don't forget your manners at the table. Mealtime should be an enjoyable moment with friends and family. Let's all be on the same playing field and learn table manners.

Life Skills Required:
- ⚜ Table Setting 101
- ⚜ Pre-Dinner Prep
- ⚜ Utensils @ Play
- ⚜ Eating Rules
- ⚜ Finish Line

Equipment needed:
- ⚜ You
- ⚜ Parents, siblings and friends to practice
- ⚜ Utensils, tableware and food

Game Directions:

- ⚜ Take the challenges
- ⚜ Have an adult check the box at the end of the game after you complete the challenge ☑
- ⚜ Cash in your tickets for the reward chosen with your coach (your parents)

Ticket Goal:_____

Game Prize:_____

TABLE SETTING 101

A pretty placemat. A nice table setting. A flower arrangement in the middle. The way you set the table can change the appearance of the food and sets the tone of the meal. At your house, you will most likely use a basic casual table setting for every day eating. When you attend formal holiday events and visit restaurants, you will see more formal settings.

You set the table with what is needed for the meal. Flatware (your utensils) is arranged

> ARRANGE FLATWARE AROUND PLATE IN THE ORDER THAT IT IS USED!

around a main plate in the order that it is used-starting at the outside and working towards the center (the main plate).

The Players and Positions

In this game, it's the utensils who are the players! Their positions and roles are detailed here.

> The first eating utensil consisted of simple sharp stones to cut meat and fruit. Spoons were made from hollow pieces of wood or seashells and connected to a stick. Animal horns were also used to drink liquids.

THE BASIC GAME PLAN

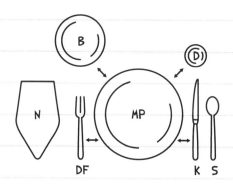

↔ **1 inch spaces between arrow positions!

The Main Plate (MP)

The plate is the main and most valuable player (MP). Everything will focus around the MP.

He is center stage on the field with players on all sides. Some times there is a saved spot for him and sometimes he makes a grand entrance! In more formal settings, he might have the napkin join him in the center.

Everything revolves around the MAIN PLATE -MP.

The Bread Plate (b)

The bread plate (b) has a side role about 1 inch diagonally next to MP. He is a supporting player for your bread. His position is on the top left side of MP. He is not always around for every meal.

TIME OUT!
Knock, Knock!
-Who's there?
Dishes
-Dishes who?
Dishes me, who are you?

The Drink Glass (d)

The drink glass (d) has a side role place on the right side one inch diagonally from MP and above the knife.

41

The Fork (DF)

The fork has a handle and the top part are the prongs. There are different type of forks. The most important fork is the dinner fork (DF). The DF is always placed about one inch away from the MP on the left side.

DF

The Knife (K)

The dinner knife is another supporting player during the meal. It has a good position on the right side about one inch away from MP. The blade faces the plate. If the main course requires a steak knife (a sharper knife), it becomes the substitute player for the dinner knife.

K

The Spoon (S)

The soup spoon is a reserve player only used when you are having soup. It takes the position next to the Knife (K). In a more formal setting you may have a dessert spoon on the top.

S

TIME OUT!
Q: What did one knife say to another?
A: You look sharp!

Additions to the Roster

Now that we understand the basic players and their positions, let's add some players to create a more formal table setting. The players include a salad fork, a dessert spoon and fork and a wine glass.

Table Setting Tricks

There's a bag of tricks for learning how to set a table and what to use first! The tried-and true-tricks:

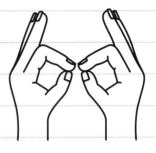

Letters b and d

Hold your hands in front of you. Touch the tips of your thumbs to the tips of your forefingers to create an 'o'. Use your left hand to make a lower case 'b'. The bread plate goes on the left side. Use your right hand to make a lower case 'd' to remind you that drinks go on the right.

Whose team are you on?

✤ Most of the items that are spelled with four letters will be to your left (L-E-F-T)

F-O-R-K, R-O-L-L

✤ Most of the items that are spelled with five letters will be on your right (R-I-G-H-T)

K-N-I-F-E, S-P-O-O-N, D-R-I-N-K

> TABLE SETTING TRICKS: THE b & d. WHOSE TEAM ARE YOU ON AND HOW FORKS CAN HELP YOU!

The word FORKS (minus the R)

The order left to right F is for fork, O for plate, K for knives, and S for spoons.

GAME CHALLENGE #1: Name 5 things that are wrong with this basic table setting:

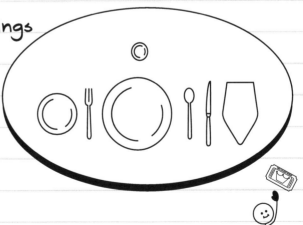

1.

2.

3.

4.

5.

PRE-DiNNER PREP

Pre-game skills prepare you for a great match! You put on your uniform, tie your shoes and warm up, and sometimes say the "Pledge of Allegiance" or sing the national anthem. Just like sports, there are rules to follow before we eat.

Basic Dress Code

> BEFORE YOU EAT. WASH YOUR HANDS AND DRESS APPROPRIATELY.

First wash your hands and dress appropriately. If you are eating inside at a table you should wear a shirt and take off your cap or hat. If your clothes are dirty, you should change them before sitting down. Obviously if you are at the beach, a casual BBQ, or a pool party you will have a different set of rules.

> WAIT TO EAT UNTIL EVERY- ONE IS SEATED! FOLLOW YOUR HOST.

Wait for the Signal...

Once you are seated, you should wait until everyone is served and the hostess (often your parents) sits down. It's always nice to begin by thanking the cook. "Thanks mom (or dad), the dinner looks really good." In some homes, you say grace before you eat. If you are invited to dine with a family that says grace, but it is not something you do at home, just politely bow your head and listen. Begin eating once you get a signal from a grown up.

RULE BREAKERS!

✣ DON'T have dirty hands at the table.

✣ DON'T sit down and start eating before everyone is seated.

✣ DON'T wear caps or hats at the table.

> **GAME CHALLENGE #2:** True or False? You should wait for everyone to be seated before beginning your meal.

Sitting Position

At the dinner table, sit up straight (even if you are tired or sick!). And never put your elbows on the table while eating. Once you are seated, stay seated quietly without squirming or rocking.

This dinner is delicious. Don't I look happy and excited to be here?

RULE BREAKERS!

✤ DON'T have 'ants in your pants' at dinner. No moving around and getting up during dinner.

✤ DON'T play with your food or your utensils, plates, bowls and cups.

SIT STILL. USE GOOD POSTURE AND NO ELBOWS ON TABLE, PLEASE!

The Napkin goes where?

The Napkin

Is it a towel? A new shirt? What is the purpose of the napkin? Before eating, the napkin should be placed on your lap and used throughout the meal. Use a gentle tap or dab to remove any bits of food that didn't quite make it into the mouth. Then place your napkin back down on your lap. If you need to leave the table during dinner, leave it on your chair. And when finished, place the napkin in the empty spot where the plate used to be or on the side.

PLACE THE NAPKIN ON YOUR LAP AND USE IT TO DAB ANY STRAY BITS OF FOOD.

RULE BREAKERS!

✤ Don't start eating before the napkin is in your lap.

✤ Don't use your sleeve or the tablecloth to replace the napkin.

✤ Don't lick your fingers to wipe off food.

✤ Don't wave the napkin in the air and attach it to yourself as a bib.

✤ Don't use the napkin as a washcloth on your face.

UTENSILS @ PLAY

Using utensils can be compared to riding a bike. If your balance is off, it won't work very well. Food won't launch off the table or spill onto your clothes if you use utensils correctly. Don't worry-it takes practice and patience!

TOP UTENSIL USAGE Plays:

✢ Use utensils on the outside first and work your way inward with each new course that is served.

✢ If you are not sure which utensil to use, wait to see what is served.

✢ Watch others at the table and follow their lead.

> WHEN USING UTENSILS FOLLOW THE OUTSIDE-IN RULE. OUTSIDE FIRST AND THEN WORK YOUR WAY INWARD.

The Grip Technique

Place utensils in your palms

> In the old days, children had to learn to hold down their elbows using a book. They had to carefully cut their food and hold down their elbows to not drop the book.

Hold out your hand and gently place the utensils in the palm of your hand. For all right-handed users, the fork should remain in the left hand and the knife is in the right hand. For all left-handed users reverse the hands. Notice that the prongs will be facing up when you place it in your palm. And the knife blade will be facing the other palm.

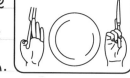

Turn your hands over

Place and keep the index finger (point the index finger) on the back of the fork and knife and then turn your palm and utensils over. The knife is in your right hand. The index finger is straight and rests near the base of the top. The sharp side is down. The other four fingers then wrap around the handle. The fork is in your left hand. The prongs face downward from you. The index finger is straight and rests on the back-side

near the head of the fork. The other four fingers wrap around the handle.

GAME CHALLENGE #3: What's the difference between a salad fork and a regular fork?

Cutting

Once you have mastered the grip, it's time to move on to cutting.

Apply sufficient pressure.

Hold the food with the fork by applying pressure to the index finger. Cut with the knife, in the same way. Keep just a little pressure to the top of the utensils while you cut.

> **HOLD THE KNIFE AND FORK CORRECTLY TO CUT WITH EASE.**

Move the knife back and forth to cut.

Apply a little bit more pressure if it's difficult to cut. Make sure to keep your elbows down!

Cut a bite size piece before eating.

Take small bites even if you are hungry or the food is difficult to cut. If it is too hard to cut, just ask a grown up for help.

With small items like rice or beans you can turn the fork over and use a scooping style. Use your knife to help scoop the pieces. Don't use your fingers as little helpers. The knife is a much better player!

RULE BREAKERS!

- ✣ DON'T hold utensils like a shovel.
- ✣ DON'T get puffy cheeks from placing too much food in your mouth.
- ✣ DON'T use your fingers or hands unless it's a finger food.
- ✣ DON'T wave your utensils around in the air.
- ✣ DON'T talk with your mouth open. No one wants to see what is inside of he mouth!
- ✣ DON"T cut the entire chicken before eating. Cut small pieces to eat one piece at a time.

Eating Styles

> CHOOSE YOUR EATING STYLE: American or Continental?

What do you do after you have finished cutting? Choose your eating style-the American style or the Continental style (also known as European style).

American Style

Three steps: 1. Cut. 2. Switch hands. 3. Eat.
Fork starts in the left hand while you cut. Then put down the knife and switch the fork to the opposite hand to eat. Let's call this play Criss Cross, Pass & Touchdown.

Continental style

Two steps: 1. Cut and 2. Eat.
Fork in the left hand and knife in the right hand. You cut and eat the food in this position. There is no switching hands. Let's call this play Zig Zag & Score.

Resting & Finished Positions

> TWO SECRET CODES: resting and finished positions for the utensils.

Just like sports, there are secret codes in the game of table manners. These codes let people know if you are resting or finished with your meal.

The Backward "V" Sign

Rest your utensils on the plate in a backward "V" to show that you are still eating. Never rest utensils on the table or the linens. This sign is often used when you eat using the Continental style. Or if you need a rest while cutting food.

49

'Time Out' American Style

Rest your knife on the top right of your plate (diagonally), if you have switched hands to the American style to eat. Then simply put the fork down if you need a break.

4:20 pm Rule

Place your fork and knife together on the plate in a 4:20 pm position to say "I am finished." The knife's blade (sharp side) should face inward and fork prongs can either be up or down.

American Style in Action

Step 1. Criss-Cross
Cut the food using a criss-cross motion. Back and forth. Back and forth.

Step 2. Pass
Switch hands! Place the fork in the right hand and leave the knife on the corner of the plate while you eat.

Step 3. Touch Down
Time to eat!

Step 4. Time Out
Time to let your fork and knife rest while you talk to your friend.

Step 5. Play is Complete
The meal is finished. Use the secret 4:20 pm code to let everyone know you are done!

Continental Style in Action

Step 1. Zig Zag & Score
Cut the food and begin eating. Do not switch hands.

Step 2. Time Out
Time to let your fork and knife rest while you talk to your friend.

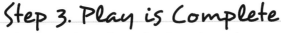

Step 3. Play is Complete
The meal is finished. Use the secret 4:20 pm code to let everyone know you are done!

Passing & Serving

Imagine driving a car on a race track. Pass the food in one direction so that dishes don't collide. The whole dish or entire bread basket should be passed. Don't throw a piece of bread across the table like a football. Traditionally the food is passed to the right. One person can also hold the dish so that the next person can take the food. Or he can just hand it to a person who then serves herself. Please don't drive the wrong way around the table!

> PASS THE WHOLE DISH IN ONE DIRECTION.

Bread & Butter

Bread is placed on the bread plate (if you have one) or on the side of your plate if you don't have one. Break off a small piece and eat one bite at a time. Don't take the whole piece of bread up to your mouth and bite off pieces. After all, we aren't dogs, trying to chew off the meat

> BREAK THE BREAD AND EAT ONE BITE AT A TIME.

from a large bone, right?

How do you butter your bread? Rest the piece of bread against your plate and butter it. Butter one piece at a time.

RULE BREAKER!

‡ Don't take the last piece of bread without first offering it to others.

‡ Don't butter the whole bread and then take bites from it.

GAME CHALLENGE #4: Which statement is NOT true?

1 There are no rules for passing and serving food.

2 Bread should be placed on the bread plate.

3 Pass the whole dish in one direction.

Water Break

Imagine a big glass of juice sitting in front of you. Now you happen to be very hungry and thirsty. You stuff a large piece of chicken into your mouth and grab the milk to wash it down. STOP! Drinking and eating should be

done separately. First chew and swallow the food. Then take a water break, making sure not to slurp or blow bubbles. Don't fill your cup so that it almost over flows. If you have a tickle or are choking, you might need a little sip of water to wash it down-a game exception!

> DRINKING AND EATING SHOULD BE DONE SEPARATELY.

Finished

In sports, everyone runs at different speeds. The same is true when we eat. When you are on the bench, you still stay and support the team. At a

> AT THE END OF A MEAL, THANK THE HOST AND ASK TO BE EXCUSED. OFFER TO HELP CLEAN UP.

meal, wait until everyone is finished and then ask to be excused. Thank your mom or host for a delicious dinner! What happens after you finish playing a tennis game? Do you just stand up and leave without cleaning up the court? When you are done with dinner, offer to help clean up the kitchen!

> GAME CHALLENGE #5: Name one good trick to use when setting the table?

Game Plan #2 - Mealtime Manners

1. Arrange flatware around the plate in the order that it is used.

2. Everything revolves around the main plate - MP.

3. Table setting tricks: 1. b and d rule, 2. Whose team are you on? 3. The word FORKS (minus the R).

4. Before you eat, wash your hands and dress appropriately.

5. Wait until everyone is seated. And follow your host.

6. Sit still. Use good posture and no elbows on the table.

7. Place the napkin in your lap and dab it on any stray bits of food.

8. When using utensils, follow the outside-in-rule: Use outside utensils first then work your way inward.

9. Hold the knife and fork correctly to cut and eat with ease.

10. Choose your eating style: American or Continental?

11. The secret codes of resting and finished positions - The backward "V", Time Out and 4:20 pm rule.

12. Pass the whole dish in one direction.

13. Break the bread and eat one bite at a time.

14. Drinking and eating should be done separately.

15. At the end of a meal, thank the host and ask to be excused. Offer to help clean up.

SMART

LET'S PRACTICE!

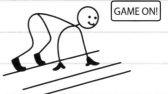

GAME ON!

SECTION 1. You make the call!

Choose DO or DON'T. Complete this section and earn 10 tickets!

1._____Eat and drink at the same time.

2._____Chew with your mouth open.

3._____Put elbows on the table.

4._____Wipe your mouth with the corners of your napkin.

5._____Sit up straight while eating.

6._____Eat and talk at the same time.

7._____Place your silverware on the table after use.

8._____Make loud noises while eating.

9._____Place your napkin in your lap before eating.

10._____Comb your hair at the table.

11._____Play video games at the table while eating.

12._____Get up from the table whenever you feel bored.

13._____Use any utensil in any order during each meal.

14._____Passing the food to the right or left is fine as long as you follow the same direction as everyone.

15._____Take food from your friend's plate.

16._____Pick food out of your teeth with your hands.

17._____Use your fingers as a knife to help push up those little pieces of rice.

18._____Hold your fork with a clenched fist because it feels comfortable.

19._____Scrape the fork or spoon against your teeth.

20._____Place your napkin on the table during dinner.

SECTION 2. Can you make the free throw? - Earn 10 tickets! ☺

1. You are eating at your friend's house for dinner. His mom lets you know that dinner is ready. What should you do?

   a. Just pick a seat.

   b. Wait for your friend or his mom to show you where to sit.

   c. Sit wherever there is an open spot.

   d. Take the usual spot that you always have at home.

2. What should you do when you first sit down at the table?

   a. Begin serving whatever food is close to you.

   b. Start a conversation.

   c. Tuck your napkin under your chin.

   d. Watch what the hostess does.

3. Mrs. Lee bows her head and says a prayer after she sits down.

   a. Just start eating.

   b. Bow your head and wait quietly.

   c. Stare at everyone.

4. You have just finished your pasta but you would like more because it was delicious! Your mom has more pasta on a serving plate. How can you get more food?

   a. Mom, will you please give me more pasta?

   b. Mom, may I please have more pasta?

   c. Can I have some more pasta?

5. Your friend comes over for dinner and begins playing with her food. She also decides to burp. What should you do?

   a. Begin playing with your food too. It looks like fun!

b. Ignore her and keep eating politely.

c. Tell her to stop because she is being very rude!

6. You are asked to pass the food. What should you do?

a. Pass the food to the right.

b. Pass it to whoever is hungry.

c. Pass it to the left.

d. Throw it across the table.

7. Your friend would like a bread roll. Just hand him a piece.

a. True

b. False

8. Circle all the correct statements about using a napkin.

a. Leave it alongside your plate so that you can see it.

b. Open it up when you sit down and place it on your lap.

c. Leave it on your chair when you are finished.

d. When finished place the napkin on your plate.

e. Tuck it under your chin.

9. Your nose starts to run during dinner. Now what should you do?

a. Just take your napkin and give it a good blow and wipe.

b. Dab your nose very discreetly and then excuse yourself to go to the bathroom.

c. Wipe your nose with your shirt sleeve.

10. What do you do if you have just taken a big bite of your food and someone asks you a question?

a. Talk with your mouth full.

b. Chew and swallow before answering.

c. Spit out your food.

11. You have just taken a bite out of your food and feel that the food is stuck in between your teeth. Now what do you do?

a. Stick your hand in your mouth and grab out the piece of food.

b. Use your fork to pick at your mouth.

c. Discreetly use your tongue to dislodge the food from your tooth.

d. Excuse yourself and use the bathroom.

12. You are really hungry and you can't seem to get the food onto your fork easily. What should you do?

a. Use your fingers to place the food onto your fork.

b. Use your fingers and stuff the food directly into your mouth.

c. Use a knife to push the food onto the fork.

13. You have just taken a bite out of the chicken and realize that a piece of bone is in your mouth. Now what do you do?

a. Spit it out on the plate and say EHHHHH!!!

b. Announce to everyone that you have a piece of bone in your mouth.

c. Discreetly use a napkin to quietly remove the piece of bone.

14. You just drank a big glass of soda and now feel the need to burp.

a. Give a loud burp.

b. Cover your mouth with a napkin and keep your mouth closed to cover up any noise.

c. Excuse yourself and go to the bathroom.

15. You have just finished eating your dinner and would like to get up and go outside. It's a beautiful day and playing outside is so much fun! What should you do?

    a. Get up and run outdoors without asking for permission and without helping with the dishes.

    b. Ask to be excused and help with the dishes quickly so that you have time to play.

    c. Ask to be excused.

16. When you are eating a piece of chicken how do you cut it?

    a. One or two pieces as you eat it.

    b. All of it before you begin.

    c. Half of it to begin with.

17. You sit down at a formal table setting and they have 3 forks placed. What should you do?

    a. Use the one you are the most comfortable with.

    b. Use the fork closest to the plate.

    c. Ask the host or waiter why you have 3 forks.

    d. Use the one farthest from your plate first.

18. You are eating dinner at a friend's house and you find a piece of hair in the food. What should you do?

    a. Yell out 'EWWW! Is that a piece of hair in my food?"

    b. Discreetly eat around the food that has the piece of hair.

    c. Eat the piece of hair. It's just a piece of hair; the food is still pretty good!

SECTION 3. Scrimmage!

Recruit family and friends to play these games.

Each game is worth one ticket. The more times you play, the more you earn.

Manners and Candies - Practice 10 different table rules:

- ✤ Rule #1 - Place the napkin on your lap
- ✤ Rule #2 - Use your utensils, NOT your fingers!
- ✤ Rule #3 - No reaching
- ✤ Rule #4 - Don't start eating until the cook is seated.
- ✤ Rule #5 - No bodily noises (slurping, burping, chewing with your mouth open, smacking your lips, etc.)
- ✤ Rule #6 - Don't leave the table until everyone has finished eating.
- ✤ Rule #7 - No elbows on the table.
- ✤ Rule #8 - No rude comments about the food.
- ✤ Rule #9 - Sit up straight and don't tip your chair.
- ✤ Rule #10 - Everyone stays to clean up the dishes and the mess!

Everyone gets a little teaser bowl or bag with small candies like M & Ms or Skittles. This will be the delicious dessert! Now the better you behave, the better chance you have to keep your dessert. Everyone has to keep an eye out to see if anyone is breaking the rules. If you break any rule you have to give a piece to the person who called you out. How much candy will you get to keep?

Fancy Dinner! - The whole family pretends that we are at a restaurant and are about to eat a formal dinner. In a sophisticated setting, we need to be dressed for the occasion and use perfect manners. Use candles and dim the lights. Make it extra special!

Set the Table Challenge - Who can set the table with all the dishes and utensils in the right place?

Secret Manner Agent - One person is assigned to be the Secret Manner Agent for the night. The secret agent will award a special dessert to the person who showed off great manner skills.

SECTION 4. Mealtime Crossword Puzzle - Earn 5 tickets! ☺

Across ☐➪

4. A utensil placed on the right hand side after the knife.

6. The _____ is placed in the middle of your table setting. A smaller version is used for the bread on the left side.

7. A style of eating with three steps - Cut, Switch Hands and Eat.

Down ⬇

1. Used for drinks and placed above the knife in a table setting.

2. A utensil placed on the right hand side of the main plate.

3. A utensil placed on the left hand side of the plate.

5. This item goes on your lap before you begin to eat.

8. A style of eating with two steps - cut and eat.

Words to Play: Plate, Knife, Fork, Spoon, Glass, American, European, Napkin

SECTION 5. Mealtime Manners Word Search – Earn 5 tickets! ☺

```
R W C N Z U O W K S E N Y L Z
T F O D Y Y W F G F M M G M N
B L N O E Q S O C T I P Q Z W
D P T N Q H R X B E T M M O D
N T I V G G S M G E L B A T Q
M F N W K I L I A V A Y Q U S
X H E A J A S M N U E K Z L K
M Z N I V J E V D I M K I S N
D X T J R R Y U A E F S P F I
K Z A P I W B Z N V N O K R F
R J L C M V B G K E O N P Q E
O N A P K I N R T N F L B T Q
F N A C S B L U E B E S E U L
R P C C J K A Q G A U Z P Y F
G N I K N I R D S S D Z G O Q
```

AMERICAN   BREAD

CONTINENTAL   DRINKING

FINISHED   FORK

KNIFE   MEALTIME

NAPKIN   SPOON

TABLE   UTENSILS

VSIGN

ANSWERS

Game Challenges:

#1) 1. Knife should be next to the plate on the right. 2. Bread plate should be diagonally top left from MP. 3. Napkin should be on the left side. 4. Soup spoon is to the right of the knife. 5. Water cup should be on the right hand side above the knife.

Formal table setting:

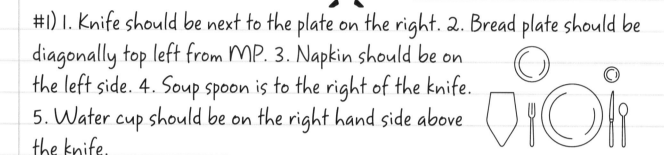

#2) True

#3) If you have a choice of two forks, you should use the fork on the outside first for the appetizer. The second fork closest to the plate is the entrée fork.

#4) 1 - There are no rules for passing and serving food.

#5) Letters b and d. Whose team are you on? The word FORKS!

Game On:

SECTION 1. You make the call!

1. Don't, 2. Don't, 3. Don't, 4. Do, 5. Do, 6. Don't, 7. Don't, 8. Don't, 9. Do, 10. Don't, 11. Don't, 12. Don't, 13. Don't, 14. Do, 15. Don't, 16. Don't, 17. Don't, 18. Don't, 19. Don't, 20. Don't.

SECTION 2. Can you make the free throw?

1. b, 2. b and/or d, 3. b, 4. b, 5. b, 6. a, 7. b. Pass the bread basket, 8. b and d, 9. b, 10. b, 11. c or d, 12. c, 13. c, 14. b or c, 15. b, 16. a, 17. d, 18. b

SECTION 3. Scrimmage!

Answers will vary. Please discuss answers with your coach (an adult).

SECTION 4. Word Search

```
+ + C + + + + + + E + + + +
+ + O D + + + + + M + + + +
+ + N + E + + + + I + + + +
+ + T N + H + + + + T + + + +
+ + I + G + S + + E L B A T +
+ + N + + I + I A + A + + + S
+ + E + + + S M N + E + + L K
+ + N + + + E V + I M + I S N
+ + T + + R + + + F S P + I
K + A + I + + + + N O + + F
R + L C + + B + + E O + + + E
O N A P K I N R T N + + + +
F N + + + + U E + + + + + +
+ + + + + + + + A + + + + +
G N I K N I R D + + D + + + +
```

(Over, Down, Direction)

AMERICAN(9,6,SW)

BREAD(7,11,SE)

CONTINENTAL(3,1,S)

DRINKING(8,15,W)

FINISHED(11,9,NW)

FORK(1,13,N)

KNIFE(15,7,S)

MEALTIME(11,8,N)

NAPKIN(2,12,E)

SPOON(14,8,SW)

TABLE(14,5,W)

UTENSILS(8,13,NE)

VSIGN(8,8,NW)

SECTION 5. Crossword Puzzle

Across ⇨ 4. Spoon   6. Plate   7. American

Down ⬇ 1. Glass   2. Knife   3. Fork   5. Napkin   8. European

TICKET TALLY SCORE BOARD

Ask an adult to place a check on a ticket after each game challenge or practice section. How many tickets were you able to collect?

Notes:

TABLE SETTING LINE UP

S

K

MP

DF

B

N

The Players......

MP – Main Plate
DF – Dinner Fork
K – Knife
S – Spoon
B – Bread Plate
D – Drink
N – Napkin

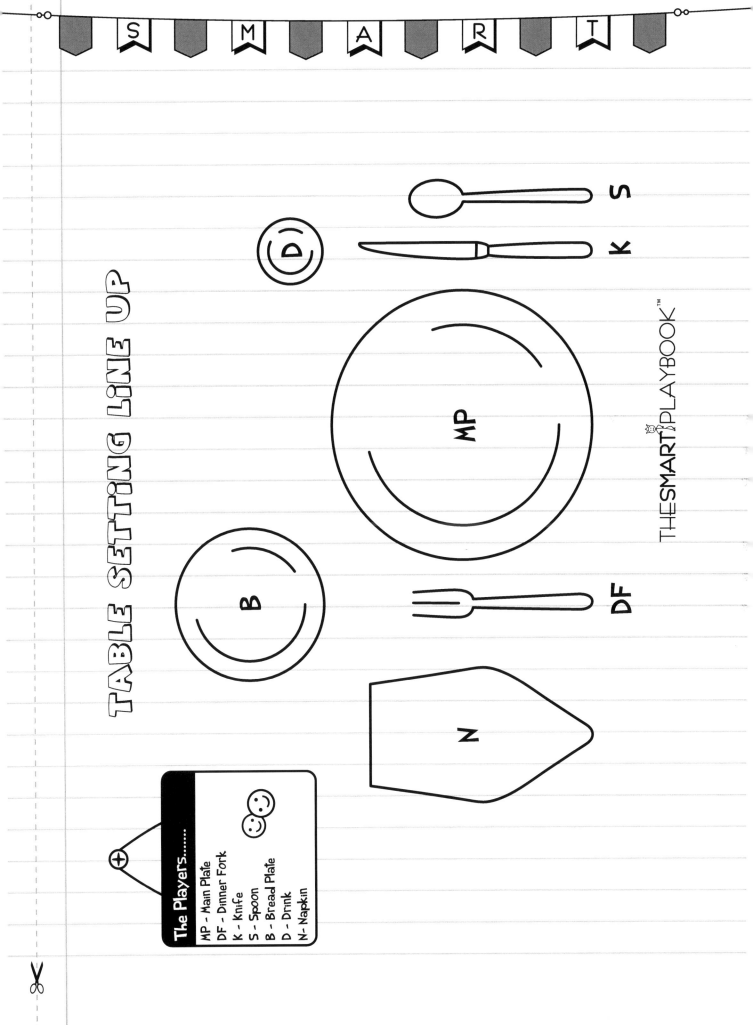

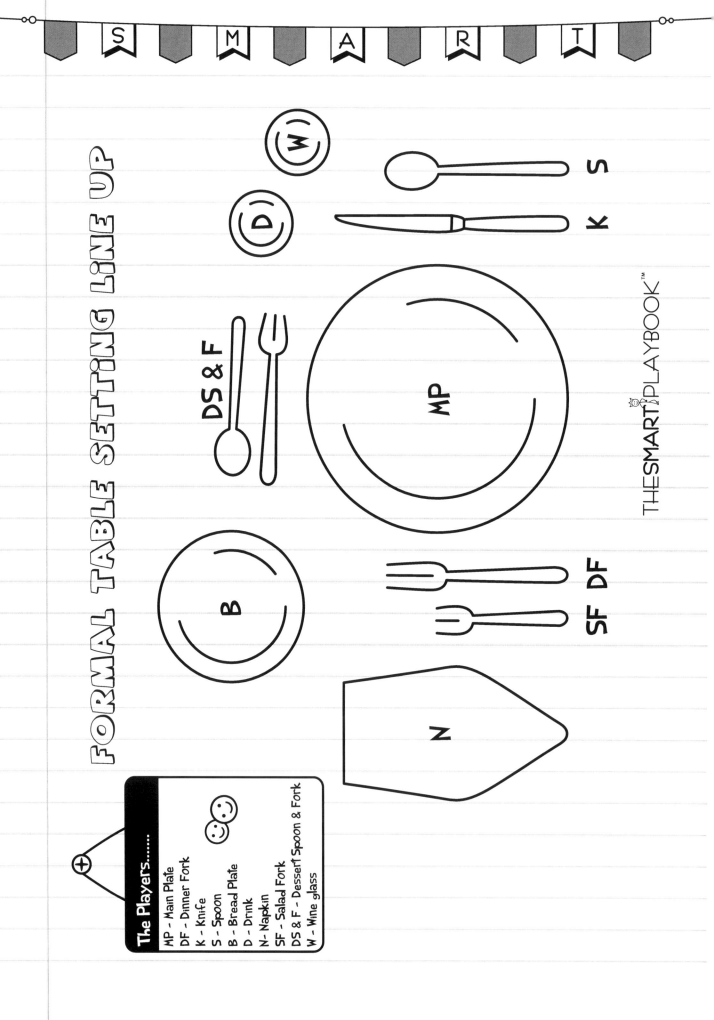

FORMAL TABLE SETTING LINE UP

The Players......

MP – Main Plate
DF – Dinner Fork
K – Knife
S – Spoon
B – Bread Plate
D – Drink
N- Napkin
SF – Salad Fork
DS & F – Dessert Spoon & Fork
W – Wine glass

W

D

DS & F

MP

B

SF   DF

N

K   S

THESMART PLAYBOOK™

GAME PLAN #3 ART OF CONVERSATION

GOAL:

How do you start a conversation with someone you've never met? With a little practice, talking with anyone can be fun and interesting. Think of it as learning to play tennis. Relax, serve, and practice. Are you ready to swing a conversation with anyone?

Life Skills Required:

- ✢ Magic Word Review
- ✢ Announcing the Players
- ✢ Body Language & Tone
- ✢ Conversation 101
- ✢ Field Map
- ✢ Forming Questions

Equipment needed:

- ✢ You
- ✢ Parents, siblings and friends to practice

Game Directions:

- ✢ Take the challenges
- ✢ Have an adult check the box at the end of the game after you complete the challenge
- ✢ Cash in your tickets for the reward chosen with your coach (your parents)

Ticket Goal:_____

Game Prize:_____

SMART

MAGIC WORD REVIEW

In all conversations there are a few key words and phrases that are important and always appropriate to use. You may have heard of them as the magic words.

Top WORD Plays:

✦ **Thank you** - What you use as a polite expression of one's gratitude.

✦ **Please** - Whenever you ask for something always insert the polite word known as "please."

✦ **You are welcome** - When someone says thank you, the right polite response is "You are welcome."

✦ **Excuse me** - Used to overcome an obstacle such as bumping into someone, burping by mistake etc.

✦ **Sorry** - A word used to apologize. A simple sorry to let someone know politely that you did not mean to do something. Also, use sorry if you can't really understand what someone is saying: "Sorry, can you repeat that?"

TIME OUT!
Knock Knock
-Who's there?
Tank
-Tank who?
You're welcome

RULE BREAKER!

✦ DON'T bump into someone and not say anything.

✦ DON'T nod or say nothing if someone thanks you. Instead, say "You are welcome."

USE POLITE WORDS AND PHRASES IN CONVERSATION.

✦ DON'T accept an apology by saying "That's okay, but it really was your fault."

GAME CHALLENGE #1: Add some magic to the following sentences:

1. _____, pass me the milk.

2. Someone hands you a cookie. Your response is_____.

3. You didn't hear what your friend just said. You say,

_____.

ANNOUNCING THE PLAYERS

Have you ever been at a big event where you run into lots of people that you know? Suddenly you are standing with Sally from soccer and Henry from baseball. Who should you introduce first? Don't worry, it takes practice and no one is going to fault you for using the wrong order. The most important thing is that you introduce people to each other.

> ALWAYS INTRODUCE PEOPLE TO EACH OTHER.

 ## Who's First?

Address the older person first.

> Mrs. Cho I'd like to introduce my friend Jeff.
> Jeff, Mrs. Cho works with my dad.

TIME OUT!

Knock Knock
-Who's there?
Annie!
-Annie who?
Annie one you like.

Address a woman before a man.

> Mrs. Jackson. I'd like to introduce you to my baseball coach, Mr. Swing.
> Coach Swing, Mrs. Jackson is my English teacher.

The first person's name you say is always the most important person.

> Coach Gallagher, this is my brother Mark.
> Mark this is my basketball coach, Mr. Gallagher.

Identify with Names

Identify the people you are introducing and use the names they'll use for each other.

Lisa. I'd like to introduce my brother Marco. Marco. Lisa is my friend from school.

Forget a Name? Come up with a creative play. Introduce the person you do know and chances are that the other person will introduce themselves.

Hi Kate. It's nice to meet you. My name is Joseph.

Let me introduce you to Kate.

Mispronounced Names. If someone mispronounces your name, it is okay to correct them. My son once spent a whole week at camp being called Charles instead of Charlie because he was afraid to correct them. A simple "I prefer Charlie," would have made him more comfortable all week.

IDENTIFY WHO YOU ARE INTRODUCING. AND USE THEIR NAME.

Hi Jane. I prefer Charlie. Nice to meet you.

GAME CHALLENGE #2

Introduce someone today. ⟹

BODY LANGUAGE & TONE

Can you figure out your opponent's next move? Everyone can communicate messages to each other without using a single word. Even when you are

> **WATCH YOUR BODY LANGUAGE WHILE SPEAKING.**

talking, your bodies are saying things too. In fact some say that 90% of your communicating comes from your body. This means that your body language is very important when talking. Sit up and stand tall. Watch your facial expression. Make eye contact! Watch hand movements. Too much arm waving while speaking is distracting. A few nods here and there makes you look interested. Continuous head bopping can make you look too excited.

A Big Smile ☺

Your smile is a powerful tool. A big smile makes you look happy and confident. The more you smile the happier you will feel.

> **USE YOUR SMILE WHILE COMMUNICATING.**

A smile makes people want to talk to you. A smile softens your voice and makes you sound warm and friendly. Always put a smile on your face while making conversation.

TIME OUT!
Knock Knock
-Who's there?
Dewey
-Dewey who?
Dewey have to keep telling these jokes!

The R.I.C.A Rule

These eyes were meant for R.I.C.A! Why use eye contact?

- ❖ **RESPECT** - Earn respect by looking people in the eye. Eye contact shows that you know what they are saying and you understand that it is important to them.

- ❖ **INTEREST** - Eye contact tells the other person that you are interested in what they are saying. Looking down or away may be misunderstood as a lack of interest.

WHILE TALKING, USE THE RICA RULE TO SHOW RESPECT, INTEREST, COMPREHENSION, AND APPRECIATION.

✤ **COMPREHEND** – To comprehend means to really understand. Eye ontact shows that you understand what they are saying.

✤ **APPRECIATION** – A meaningful look into someone's eyes says that you really mean it.

GAME CHALLENGE #3: Let's play charades. Strike the following pose using just your body to communicate a feeling. Have your parents guess what you are trying to act out!

✤ Bored

✤ Angry

✤ Shy

✤ Happy

Personal Space

A comfortable conversation takes place in a comfortable place. Be aware that not everyone feels comfortable talking face to face very close. Most people prefer to be about eighteen inches away from someone when talking. That's about as long as your arm.

A little too close!

RULE BREAKERS!

✤ DON'T frown while talking to someone.

✤ DON'T look at the ground when you speak.

✤ DON'T cross your arms when speaking to someone–it can make you look angry.

✤ DON'T stand too close to someone while speaking.

✤ Don't mumble when talking. Speak clearly.

RESPECT PERSONAL SPACE WHILE HAVING A CONVERSATION.

GAME CHALLENGE #4:

Write who you would feel comfortable talking to in each empty area?

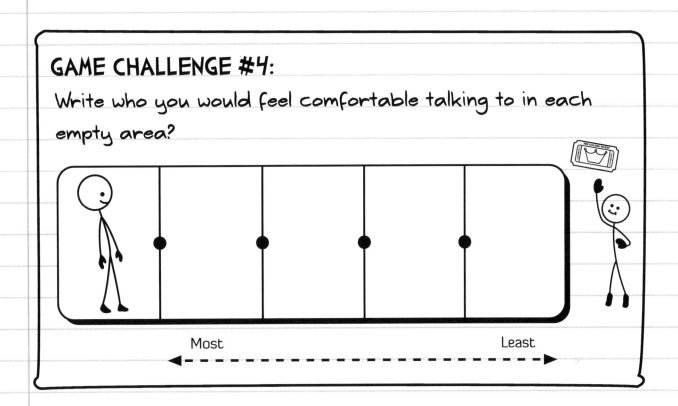

Most

Least

Tone?

I am happy!

How things are said can be just as important as what is said. Your tone can sometimes give a stronger message than your voice. The way you say it can actually completely change the meaning of what you say.

> WATCH YOUR TONE WHEN SPEAKING!

GAME CHALLENGE #5: Does the voice tone affect the meaning of what is said? Say the following phrases with a different tone:

✣ I have so much homework. (happy) (sad) (surprised)

✣ I think your haircut looks great! (happy) (sad) (surprised)

✣ I love to play baseball. (happy) (sad) (bored)

Volume Control

Pretend that your voice is a speaker that you can turn up and down. Adjust the volume of your voice from soft to loud depending on the situation. Using the wrong volume can make others uncomfortable. Choose the appropriate one.

> ADJUST THE VOLUME OF YOUR VOICE DEPENDING ON THE SITUATION.

GAME CHALLENGE #6: Circle the right voice volume for each situation:

1. Studying in a library	Soft	Normal	Loud
2. On the school bus	Soft	Normal	Loud
3. Talking in the lunchroom	Soft	Normal	Loud
4. Watching a movie	Soft	Normal	Loud
5. Playing outdoors	Soft	Normal	Loud

SMART

CONVERSATION 101

Conversation is all about the back-and-forth. Don't be shy. Be bold. Ask a question to break the silence.

Get the Ball Moving

Top START-Talk Plays

1. Introduce yourself.
2. Use any information you have already been told about the person.
3. Ask a question. Don't just ask a 'yes' or 'no' question. Use questions with who, what, where, when and more. This will help you get a response with more detail and open the door for more questions.
4. Tell them a little bit about yourself.
5. Give them a nice compliment. For example, "I really like your dress."

> THE FIRST STEP TO A CONVERSATION IS TO GET THE BALL GOING!

GAME CHALLENGE #7: Change the below questions to ones that will keep the conversation going.

1. Do you like pizza?
2. Who is your favorite baseball team?
3. Do you live in town?

Keep It Interesting....

Everyone loves to have others show interest in them. You can show interest through questions and compliments. Who is your favorite player? What team did you play for? Does your dad like baseball? Always have topics and questions ready. When a conversation begins to run out, you can always say " Did you hear about ......" and share something interesting.

> SHOW INTEREST IN THE OTHER PERSON.

- The weather
- A baseball game
- A holiday event
- A great book
- A new movie
- Something interesting that happened in school

GAME CHALLENGE #8: You meet a new person at school. Write three possible conversation topics. Ready, set, go....

1.

2.

3.

Talking Tennis Match

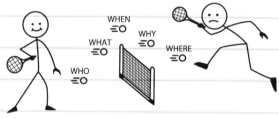

Tennis anyone? A conversation is like a tennis ball going back and forth. You take turns. You say something, perhaps a question or a thought, and then the other person comes back with a reply or another thought. You go back and forth. Well-matched players and balanced play make tennis-and talking-fun! The best way to keep the conversation going is to **listen!** Look for common interests or friends. Talk about an event or what is happening around you. There's always a way to find something in common no matter how different you might be. Listen carefully. Show interest.

THINK OF A CONVERSATION AS A TENNIS BALL GOING BACK AND FORTH.

Do **not interrupt.** If you have to interrupt, use the polite words "excuse me." **Be yourself.** Don't lie or pretend that you are something that you are not.

LISTEN. BE YOURSELF AND DO NOT INTERRUPT WHILE TALKING.

Fumbles and Fillers

Sometimes when your brain is searching for the next words to say, your mouth keeps going and blurts out meaningless words, sounds and phrases.

+ Fumble Sounds - um, uh, ah, mm, err, oh
+ Fumble Words - basically, actually, literally, like
+ Filler Phrases - "I think that," "you know," "what I'm trying to say is…"

Fillers and fumbles make you appear less confident. Before you speak, you must think, "This is what I am going to say," and then when you start to speak, say it clearly!

> LOSE THE FUMBLE AND FILLERS BY SLOWING DOWN AND STAYING ON TOPIC.

SLOW DOWN the pace and work on accuracy.

If you are playing baseball, it's better to pause and think where you should throw the ball. If you just randomly throw, you probably won't make a smart play.

TIME OUT - Use the pause to reduce the fumble and fillers. Replace them with silence.

STAY ON TOPIC - Do not skip around to different subjects.

DO NOT INTERRUPT - Imagine if you ran up to the net to distract your opponent when he was serving.

RULE BREAKERS!

+ DON'T talk about how much money you have and what something costs.
+ DON'T use slang words such as "yeah" or "nah" when speaking with an adult.

> **GAME CHALLENGE #9:** Pick any topic. Think about what you would like to say. Record yourself. Were you able to avoid fumbles and fillers? Try again.

Talk with Empathy

Empathy is the ability to experience another person's

emotions. Let's say you are talking to your friend and can tell by her expressions that she is very sad. Since we are face-to-face, we can look beyond our needs and show her some empathy while we chat.

Top EMPATHY Plays:

* Play detective - Read people's faces to understand how they are feeling.
* Listen - Show the other person that you understand. Repeat what they just said. "What I hear you saying is..."
* Show Empathy - Accept what your friend is feeling regardless of whether you agree with them or not. "I can see why you would feel upset...."

GAME CHALLENGE #10: Put Empathy to Play! Your friend is upset because she thinks that you didn't include her in a game. How could you respond to make her feel better? Circle the best answer.

1) I have no idea why you are upset.
2) I can see how you might think that we didn't include you but we didn't realize that you wanted to play with us.
3) You are right. We did not want you to play with us.

Out-of-Bounds Talk

There are certain ways to act and talk when you don't know what to say. If you don't like something, it is often better to leave it unsaid than be rude. Here's your chance to apply tact and courtesy to a conversation.

Situation: Your friend is eating a sandwich that you think looks gross!

Bad: Saying something negative about the sandwich.

Good: You choose to say nothing and let him finish the sandwich.

RULE BREAKERS!

✢ DON'T use inappropriate language.

✢ DON'T make jokes in a serious situation.

✢ DON'T ignore people's emotions.

> USE THE WHO, WHAT, WHERE, WHEN, WHY AND HOW QUESTIONS.

Forming Questions?

Get the ball rolling with a great talking question, also known as the WHO, WHAT, WHERE, WHEN, WHY & HOW technique.

WHO	A person
WHAT	A thing or action. Books, sports, games, running, drawing etc.
WHERE	A place. Playground, sports practice, the bus etc.
WHEN	A time. Night, day, season, time, date etc.
WHY	A reason.
HOW	Details....

Tell me three things you remember from kindergarten?

If you could trade lives with somebody you know. who would it be?

What kids are popular in your grade? What makes someone popular?

What is your favorite sport and why?

When is your birthday?

Do you have any brothers or sisters?

What is your favorite color?

What is your favorite subject? Why?

Which of your friends are you the proudest of?

If you could change three things about yourself, what would they be?

Do you ride the bus?

What grade are you in?

What school do you go to?

What do you do during recess?

What is your least favorite subject in school? Why?

Do you play a musical instrument?

How do you like riding the bus?

If you could change the world. Name two things you would like to change? Why?

When do you like to work on your homework?

GAME CHALLENGE #11: How many questions can you think of?
BONUS: Earn 5 tickets!

GAME CHALLENGE #12: Use questions to keep a conversation going. Pick a friend and fill out the sheet below. Read your parts and then keep the conversation going....

You: I have a dog.   Your partner: What is her name?

You: Lola   Your partner: What kind of a dog?

You: A black lab   Your partner:

You: Your partner:

You: Your partner:

You:

FIELD MAP

Imagine a conversation is like a football field with a successful conversation equal to a TOUCHDOWN! You start with a greeting and then with each exchange, you get a first down. At the fifty-yard line, you're halfway through the conversation, taking turns with the ball. Then as you approach the end of the conversation you head for the end zone. TOUCHDOWN!

Top FIELD MAP Plays:

1. LISTEN more than you talk. Nod your head to show that you are listening and even throw in fumble words - hmm, uh-huh.
2. PREPARE with a lot of different ideas for topics and questions to talk about.
3. TAKE TURNS while speaking.
4. THINK before you speak.
5. Use the MAGIC WORDS.

> GREAT CONVERSATION TAKES PRACTICE. MAP OUT YOUR PLAN.

RULE BREAKERS!

✦ DON'T interrupt.
✦ DON'T talk to only one person when speaking in a group.
✦ DON'T overshare too much information.
✦ DON'T brag.
✦ DON'T pretend to be listening.

> TOP PLAYS INCLUDE: LISTEN, PREPARE, TAKE TURNS, THINK AND USE THE MAGIC WORDS.

GAME CHALLENGE #13: The 'After You' conversation Play. Both you and your friend start to speak at the same time. What should you do?

1. Speak a little louder and more forcefully so that your friend understands that you intend to speak first.
2. Use the 'After You' play so that your friend can go first and then you will wait to take your turn.
3. Decide to not speak at all.

FIELD MAP #1

Basic Talk Training

1st DOWN - GAME START
+ Hi
+ What's new?
+ How are you?
+ My name is …

2nd DOWN - CONTINUE WITH COMMENT OR QUESTION?
+ What are you doing?
+ I just heard something funny.
+ Let me tell you….
+ Where are you from?

3rd DOWN - TALKING
+ Take turns.
+ Both should be talking about the SAME topic.
+ Don't interrupt.
+ Use the WHO, WHAT, WHERE, WHY questions.
+ LISTEN.
+ Make positive comments.

4th DOWN - SHORT EXPLANATION TO WRAP IT UP.
+ "I better go now…"
+ "I didn't realize it was so late. I have to run."
+ "Have a nice day."
+ "Nice to see you."

TOUCH DOWN = GOODBYE

Goal 10 20 30 40 50 40 30 20 10 Goal

Goal 10 20 30 40 50 40 30 20 10 Goal

FIELD MAP #2

Meeting Someone New

1st DOWN - GAME START - Decide if it is a good time to walk up to a person. Introduce yourself. Ask for their name.

You: Hi, I'm Nicky. What's your name?

New Person: I'm Charlie.

You: It's nice to meet you, Charlie. That's a great name. I have a brother named Charlie.

2nd DOWN - CONTINUE COMMENT OR QUESTION?

If you are at the same birthday party, you can ask how they know the host. Here's your chance to be a detective and figure out how to keep the conversation going. Ask lots of questions and show interest. Listen.

3rd DOWN - TALKING

Take turns. Both should be talking about the SAME topic. Do not interrupt. Use the WHO, WHAT, WHERE, WHY, HOW question. And remember to keep them as OPEN questions.

What school do you go to? Do you play any sports? How old are you? Where do you live, What's your favorite sports team?

4th DOWN - SHORT EXPLANATION TO WRAP IT UP.

"I better go now...", "I didn't realize it was so late, I have to run."

TOUCH DOWN = GOODBYE

GAME CHALLENGE #14: You are at a birthday party and you sit down next to someone you have never met. What do you do? Fill in the field map.

1st DOWN - GAME START

_____

_____

2nd DOWN - START WITH A COMMENT OR QUESTION

_____

3rd DOWN - TALKING

_____

_____

4th DOWN - SHORT EXPLANATION TO WRAP IT UP

_____

_____

TOUCH DOWN = GOODBYE

Game Plan #3 - Art of Conversation

1. Use polite words and phrases in a conversation.
2. Always introduce people to each other.
3. Identify who you are introducing by using their name.
4. Watch your body language while speaking.
5. Use your smile while communicating.
6. While talking, use the RICA rule to show respect, interest, comprehension and appreciation.
7. Respect personal space while having a conversation.
8. Tone awareness is very important when speaking.
9. Adjust the volume of your voice depending on the situation.
10. The first step to a conversation is to get the ball going.
11. Show interest in the other person.
12. Think of conversation as a tennis ball going back and forth.
13. Listen, be yourself and do not interrupt while talking.
14. Lose fumble and filler words by slowing down and staying on topic.
15. Empathy is the ability to experience other people's emotions.
16. Use the WHO, WHAT, WHERE, WHY & HOW questions.
17. Great conversation techniques take practice - map out your plan.
18. Top field map plays: listen, prepare, take turns, think and use the magic words.

LET'S PRACTICE!

GAME ON!

SECTION 1. You make the call!

Fill in DO or DON'T. Complete this section and earn 10 tickets!

1. _____ Your friend just came to your party and gave you a gift. You grab it and give her a nod.

2. _____ Your brother apologized for breaking your new video game. You reply, "Okay, I forgive you."

3. _____ You bump into someone in the hallway and she trips. You yell, "Hey! Watch where you are going!"

4. _____ Jane meets Joe for the first time. She smiles brightly, stands tall and introduces herself.

5. _____ Joe talks to Nicky while looking down at his feet.

6. _____ When meeting someone for the first time show interest.

7. _____ Sandy is sharing a story with a friend. "Um, Uh, Jane would like to, you know, share a like story with her class. What I'm trying to say...."

8. _____ Create a conversation Field Map in your mind when talking to someone.

9. _____ You are talking in a large group. John is talking about football. Jill doesn't really understand football. You try to include her in the conversation by explaining that he is talking about the big game last weekend.

10. _____ You are at a family dinner party. Your mom's friend asks if you like baseball. Your response is "Yeah."

SECTION 2. Scrimmage!

Recruit family and friends to play these games.
Each game is worth one ticket. The more times you play, the more you earn.

Talking Challenge - Find a partner. Start with easy topics and then challenge yourself and pick something you know very little about.

- A favorite tennis player
- The weather tomorrow
- Favorite sport
- Favorite band
- The color red versus blue
- Living in California or a state you don't know.
- Eating a gummy worm, a cupcake, spinach etc

Roll the Ball - Practice with a sibling or a parent how to get the ball rolling in a conversation. Pretend that you just met someone for the first time. Use a ball and roll it back and forth while you talk. Each time you have the ball you need to talk. Practice listening, taking turns, showing interest.

In Style Dining - Time to bring back the simple dinner party conversation. Pick a topic once a week. The whole family should participate. Then schedule a day to talk about the topic. Everyone should research and prepare. Share and have a fun exciting dinner conversation around your chosen subject. Fun for the entire family!

Role Play

+ A friend of your parents is visiting your home. Introduce yourself.
+ A new boy or girl moves into the neighborhood. Introduce yourself.
+ You are bringing a new friend home. Show how you introduce your friend and parents to each other.
+ There is a new student in your classroom. Introduce yourself.
+ You are visiting your cousin who lives in Europe. You have just arrived at their house after a long flight from the United States. How do we start the converstion?

Tone it Up - Use different ways of saying the statements below - sad, mad, angry, happy, say it loud and now whisper. Which tone did you like?

+ Thanks for dinner, Mom!
+ I am really sorry that I spilled the cereal on the floor.
+ May I please have another cookie?

Open Sesame! Can you change a question from just a closed-end question (yes or no answer) to an open-ended question?

+ Did you have a good day?
+ Did you have fun in school today?
+ Did you like playing with Annie?
+ Do you like baseball?

Detective Talk Have a friend talk about himself for five minutes. Can you come up with five interesting topics that you think he might like after listening to him? Listen carefully and try to uncover clues.

SECTION 3. Art of Conversation Crossword Puzzle.
- Earn 5 tickets! ☺

Across 👉

3. Fumble words that should be avoided when talking.

4. A word used to apologize.

7. Always _____ people to each other.

8. A polite expression of one's gratitude.

Down 🔽

1. Who, What, Why, Where, When

2. The ability to experience other people's emotions.

5. Show respect, interest, comprehension and appreciation when talking to someone.

6. Your_____ can sometimes give a stronger message than your voice.

Words to Play: Empathy, Questions, Fillers, Thanks, Sorry, Introduce, RICA, Tone

SECTION 4. Art of Conversation Word Search - Earn 5 tickets! ☺

```
C R L D H S L E B T F C A B L
Y O X I T E V V W S M J P O O
N A M H S I W Y T E K S Q D F
T X I U T T F A Q R E M A Y J
S N O I T S E U Q E C Q D L T
K D S D X X P N M T N U X A Z
H O A C I R M A I N T O W N L
P W N G M O G N M I V V T G R
T W E I U Z T I O D I D A U L
C V D O M R U H O O L N S A H
B M M J O X Y J F J D E M G L
J X S D N D A F T L K P I E D
W J U A Y K N A T U R A L F L
C C H Y F Y M H O A C I E B U
E L Q L W L Y U K Q H I N K A
```

BODY LANGUAGE	FIELD MAP
INTEREST	INTRODUCE
LISTEN	NATURAL
POSITIVE	QUESTIONS
RICA	SMILE
THINK	TONE

S M A R T

ANSWERS

Game Challenges:

#1) 1. Please, 2. Thank you, 3. Sorry, could you repeat that.

#2) Use the 'Who's First' tips!

#3) How's your acting?

#4) Answers will vary. Talk to your coach.

#5) How's your tone?

#6) 1. Soft, 2. Normal, 3. Normal, 4. Soft, 5. Loud

#7) 1. What kind of pizza do you like to eat?, 2. Tell me about your favorite baseball team. 3. Where in town do you live?

#8) Answers will vary.

#9) Use your computer, IPAD or smartphone to record yourself. Good luck!

#10) 2

#11) Answers will vary. Talk to your coach.

#12) Answers will vary. Talk to your coach.

#13) 2

#14) Answers will vary. Talk to your coach.

Game On:

SECTION 1. You make the call!

1. Don't, 2. Do, 3. Don't, 4. Do, 5. Don't, 6. Do, 7. Don't, 8. Do, 9. Do, 10. Don't.

SECTION 2. Scrimmage

Answers will vary. Please discuss answers with your coach (an adult).

SECTION 3. Crossword Puzzle

Across ➡   3. Fillers   4. Sorry   7. Introduce   8. Thanks

Down ⬇   1. Questions   2. Empathy   5. RICA   6. Tone

SECTION 4. Word Search

```
+  +  L  +  +  +  +  E  +  T  +  +  +  B  +
+  +  +  I  T  +  V  +  +  S  +  +  +  O  +
+  +  +  H  S  I  +  +  +  E  +  +  +  D  +
+  +  I  +  T  T  +  +  +  R  +  +  +  Y  +
S  N  O  I  T  S  E  U  Q  E  +  +  +  L  +
K  +  S  +  +  +  P  N  +  T  N  +  +  A  +
+  O  A  C  I  R  +  A  I  N  +  O  +  N  +
P  +  +  +  +  +  N  M  I  +  +  T  G  +
+  +  +  +  +  +  T  +  +  D  +  +  +  U  +
+  +  +  +  +  R  +  +  +  +  L  +  S  A  +
+  +  +  +  O  +  +  +  +  +  +  E  M  G  +
+  +  +  D  +  +  +  +  +  +  +  +  I  E  +
+  +  U  +  +  +  N  A  T  U  R  A  L  F  +
+  C  +  +  +  +  +  +  +  +  +  +  E  +  +
E  +  +  +  +  +  +  +  +  +  +  +  +  +  +
```

(Over, Down, Direction)

BODYLANGUAGE(14,1,S)

FIELDMAP(14,13,NW)

INTEREST(10,8,N)

INTRODUCE(9,7,SW)

LISTEN(3,1,SE)

NATURAL(7,13,E)

POSITIVE(1,8,NE)

QUESTIONS(9,5,W)

RICA(6,7,W)

SMILE(13,10,S)

THINK(5,2,SW)

TONE(13,8,NW)

TiCKET TALLY SCORE BOARD

Have an adult place a check after each game challenge. Feel free to repeat different challenges to earn more tickets. How many tickets were you able to collect?

SCORE BOARD
X · X · X

THE GOLDEN TICKET	THE GOLDEN TICKET	THE GOLDEN TICKET	THE GOLDEN TICKET	THE GOLDEN TICKET
THE GOLDEN TICKET	THE GOLDEN TICKET	THE GOLDEN TICKET	THE GOLDEN TICKET	THE GOLDEN TICKET
THE GOLDEN TICKET	THE GOLDEN TICKET	THE GOLDEN TICKET	THE GOLDEN TICKET	THE GOLDEN TICKET
THE GOLDEN TICKET	THE GOLDEN TICKET	THE GOLDEN TICKET	THE GOLDEN TICKET	THE GOLDEN TICKET
THE GOLDEN TICKET	THE GOLDEN TICKET	THE GOLDEN TICKET	THE GOLDEN TICKET	THE GOLDEN TICKET
THE GOLDEN TICKET	THE GOLDEN TICKET	THE GOLDEN TICKET	THE GOLDEN TICKET	THE GOLDEN TICKET
THE GOLDEN TICKET	THE GOLDEN TICKET	THE GOLDEN TICKET	THE GOLDEN TICKET	THE GOLDEN TICKET
THE GOLDEN TICKET	THE GOLDEN TICKET	THE GOLDEN TICKET	THE GOLDEN TICKET	THE GOLDEN TICKET
THE GOLDEN TICKET	THE GOLDEN TICKET	THE GOLDEN TICKET	THE GOLDEN TICKET	THE GOLDEN TICKET

99

Notes:

SMART

DiY CONVERSATION CARDS

Perk up your family talk! Just cut out the cards. Create the family talk jar. One person picks a card and everyone can answer the same question or everyone can pick their own. Listen and take turns.

SEASONS OF THE YEAR
What is your favorite season? Why? Do you know an interesting fact about your favorite season? Name a fun family activity during this season?

FAVORITE SPORTS
What is your favorite sport? Who is your favorite player? Who is your favorite team? What's an interesting fact?

PLAN A DREAM VACATION
Where would you go on a dream vacation? Who would come? What would you do? Why? What's an interesting fact about your choice?

FAVORITE CANDY
What type of candy do you like to eat? What would happen if you ate tons of candy every day?

EXERCISE IMPORTANT
Why should we exercise? What are some forms of exercising? How many times a week should we exercise? What is your favorite type of exercise? What is your least favorite exercise?

SUPERPOWERS
If you could have any superpower, which would you choose? Why?

ANIMAL
If you could be an animal, what would you be and why?

YOUR FAVORITE THING
What is one thing you couldn't live without? Why?

FAME FOR 10 SECONDS
If you had the attention of the world for 10 seconds, what would you say? Why?

BEST HOLIDAY
What is your favorite holiday to celebrate? Why?

INTERESTING FACTS ABOUT YOU
Name three interesting things about you?

TEACH A CLASS FOR A DAY
If you had to teach a class for a day, what subject would you choose? What would you do?

THESMART PLAYBOOK™

GAME PLAN #4 - RESTAURANT BEHAVIOR

GOAL:

Everyone enjoys going out to a restaurant every now and then. There are five main differences between eating at your house and at a restaurant. Bon Appétit!

　　1. There is a dress code.

　　2. Your meal is served by a waiter.

　　3. You make choices and order your meal.

　　4. Other people and families are there and your behavior affects every one around you.

Life Skills Required:
　✤ The Uniform
　✤ Who's Who?
　✤ Ordering 101
　✤ Challenge Foods
　✤ Basic Manners @ the Restaurant

Equipment needed:
　✤ You
　✤ Parents, siblings and friends to practice
　✤ Utensils, tableware and food

Game Directions:
　✤ Take the challenges
　✤ Have an adult check the box at the end of the game after you complete the challenge
　✤ Cash in your tickets for the reward chosen with your coach (your parents)

Ticket Goal:_____

Game Prize:_____

S M A R T

THE UNIFORM

How many times have your parents asked you to change your clothes because you are going to a nice restaurant? What you wear makes a statement about yourself and how other people see you. The key is to match your look with the place or situation you are in.

Our Dress Options?

Informal - Fast-food and diners often fit the informal restaurant category. There is a very casual

> MATCH YOUR LOOK WITH THE PLACE OR SITUATION.

"come as you are" dress code. There are, of course, limits to this. Wear shoes unless you are at the beach. Remove baseball caps when inside and always when eating. Be clean and presentable-don't go out to eat after a long workout or game dripping with sweat and smelling. No pajamas or bathrobe unless it's a pajama party!

> DRESS OPTIONS - INFORMAL. CASUAL. BUSINESS CASUAL.CASUAL ELEGANT AND FORMAL

Casual - Casual means comfortable yet presentable. A little more formal than a typical Saturday morning 'just out of bed look'. Avoid sweats or dirty or ripped clothing. A clean shirt with jeans is perfect.

Business Casual - Adults use this term. Dress is comfortable but presentable-something they would wear to work. If you are going somewhere with your parents, this means a little more formal than jeans and a t-shirt. Maybe wear a polo shirt and nice pants or a casual skirt and top.

Casual Elegant - Dress to impress! The dressy version of casual. Boys might wear a blazer with a pair of nice pants. Girls can wear a pretty dress and party shoes.

Formal - Dress to impress to the max! Sometimes a restaurant requires a very formal dress code. Some might say "Jacket and tie required." The idea here is to take you out of your everyday life and transform your dining experience to something extraordinary!

104

GAME CHALLENGE #1: Based on the described outfit, what type of restaurant could you visit? There could be more than one answer. Discuss with your parents.

✛ Bathing suit & flip flops:

✛ Suit and tie:

✛ Party dress and shoes:

✛ Jeans or skirt and sneakers:

✛ Jeans and a collared shirt:

✛ Sundress and party shoes:

✛ Shorts and a t-shirt:

> ADJUST YOUR MANNERS ACCORDING TO THE TYPE OF RESTAURANT.

Size Up the Restaurant

Casual or formal restaurant?

TIME OUT!
Q: Why did the golfer wear two pairs of pants?
A: In case he got a Hole in One!

Adjust our manners and dress option according to the type of restaurant. The easiest way is to rate a restaurant from low to high using a star system. The more stars you give it, the more formal dress code and manners. A beach concession stand might be one star and a very formal restaurant rates as five stars.

Very casual   Very Formal

GAME CHALLENGE #2: What style of service best fits the description?

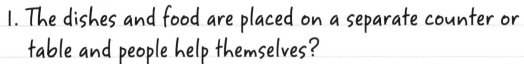

1. The dishes and food are placed on a separate counter or table and people help themselves?

   A) Family style B) Buffet style C) Restaurant style D) Fast Casual

2. The individual plates are prepared in the kitchen and brought out to the people.

   A) Family style B) Buffet style C) Restaurant style D) Fast Casual

3. The table is set and the dishes of food are placed on the table for people to serve themselves.

   A) Family style B) Buffet style C) Restaurant style D) Fast Casual

TIME OUT!
Q: Why did the cranberries turn red?
A: They saw the salad dressing.

RULE BREAKER!

❖ DON'T arrive in shorts and a t-shirt to a more formal restaurant.

❖ DON'T ignore the dress code rules. If your parents tell you to wear a jacket and tie, you need to wear one.

GAME CHALLENGE #3: Restaurant Rank? Can you rank the restaurant?

1. The table setting has a white tablecloth, beautiful china and utensils. The waiter comes over and says, "May I take your order..."

   ★   ★★   ★★★   ★★★★   ★★★★★

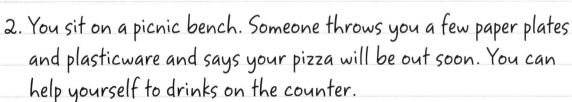

2. You sit on a picnic bench. Someone throws you a few paper plates and plasticware and says your pizza will be out soon. You can help yourself to drinks on the counter.

   ★   ★★   ★★★   ★★★★   ★★★★★

WHO'S WHO?

There are many people who work in a restaurant. Our role as a customer is to be respectful and courteous to them and to the people around us.

The Host

The host manages the tables in the restaurant. They take the reservations and make sure that they don't have too many people eating at the

> BE RESPECTFUL AND COURTEOUS TO EVERYONE THAT WORKS IN THE RESTAURANT AND THE PEOPLE AROUND US.

same time. Customers need to show up on time so that they don't interfere with other reservations. It's the same idea as showing up on time for soccer practice or a game. There's someone scheduled to play after you so we need to respect our scheduled time. Unless it's a fast food place or a very casual restaurant most places have a host.

> THE HOST'S JOB IS TO GREET YOU AT THE DOOR AND SEAT YOU AT YOUR TABLE.

Sometimes a reservation ahead of you is running late (just as a game might run into overtime) and then you will need to wait before being seated. Please be quiet and respectful as you wait patiently.

> **TIME OUT!**
> Q: What sport does a waiter love?
> A: Tennis, because they can serve so well.

The Waiter

This is the person who takes your order and serves the food. They will inform you of any special meals offered and of any other information you need to know, like if the restaurant has run out of something. As a customer, you can ask questions to the waiter about the menu and also make him aware of how you would like your food cooked.

> THE WAITER SERVES YOU THROUGHOUT YOUR MEAL.

The Bus Boy

The bus boy helps to serve water and also clear your dishes. As a customer, you usually do not disturb the bus boy. He helps the waiter make sure you have a clean table and filled water glasses.

BE RESPECTFUL TO EVERYONE THAT WORKS IN THE RESTAURANT.

TIME OUT!

Q: What did the angry customer give to the Italian waiter?

A: A pizza his mind.

ORDERING 101

When you eat in a restaurant, it's important to know how to read the menu and talk to your waiter. Don't just sit on the sidelines, jump in and learn the rules!

> THE MENU ORGANIZES THE FOOD INTO DIFFERENT COURSES.

The Menu

Menus are divided into sections for different types of food or courses. Your meal might include an appetizer, soups, salads, entrées, desserts and a drink (sometimes referred to as a beverage).

* *
* 1. Appetizer or Starter - The small dish before your main course.
     This might include a soup or salad.
* 2. Entrée - The main course.
* 3. Dessert - A sweet treat at the end of the meal.
* 4. Drinks - Drinks available.
* *

Big Foodie Words

> LEARN THE BIG FOODIE WORDS TO UNDERSTAND RESTAURANT TALK.

THE WORD	THE DEFINITION
A la carte	Foods are priced separately
Prix Fixe	A fixed price for two to three courses
Specials	Added special dishes created just for the day or evening
Early Bird Special	special price if you eat in the early evening, usually before 6:30 pm
Pre-Theater Specials	A special menu offered at restaurants before a performance
Au Gratin	Browned and buttered bread crumbs with cheese
Au Jus	French for 'in juice,' describes meats served in its own juices
Alfredo	Pasta served in a white sauce made with cream, butter and cheese
Cacciatore	Italian for a chicken cooked in a spicy tomato sauce
Hors D'oeuvres	Small dishes usually served as an appetizer
Bouillon	A thin broth or soup
Bechamel	A white sauce
Crepe	Thin pancakes

GAME CHALLENGE #4: What does the word Alfredo mean on a menu?

The Starting Play

> WHEN ORDERING, BE DECISIVE. SPEAK CLEARLY AND POLITELY.

1. Make a decision! The first question the waiter generally asks is, "What would you like to drink?" He may also ask you if you have any questions regarding the menu. The waiter usually takes the kids' drink orders first and then moves to the ladies and finally the men. He will try to go from the left to right moving clockwise.

2. Place your Order. The waiter will then come back and ask if you are ready to order. Wait until he looks at you. He will choose someone to start ordering and then go around the table.

3. Be Polite! Always say "Please" and "Thank you."

4. Speak clearly and be specific. Tell the waiter any specific requests that you might have. For example, you might prefer to have your salad with the dressing on the side. How you would like the steak cooked? The range of levels of cooked meat vary from rare to well-done.

   ✣ Rare - Most pink   ✣ Medium Rare - Slightly pink
   ✣ Medium - A hint of pink   ✣ Medium Well - Mostly brown
   ✣ Well-done - brown

5. Wait patiently. Feel free to eat the bread and drink your beverage while you wait. Enjoy!

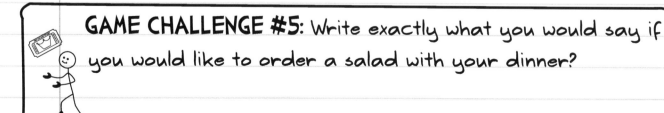

GAME CHALLENGE #5: Write exactly what you would say if you would like to order a salad with your dinner?

The Signals
Do you know the secret restaurant signals?

Signal #1 - Ready to Order. Closing your menu tells the waiter that you are ready to order.

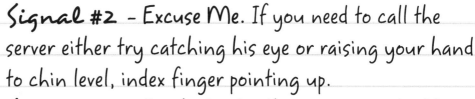

Signal #2 - Excuse Me. If you need to call the server either try catching his eye or raising your hand to chin level, index finger pointing up.

Signal #3 - Finished. Use the 4:20 pm rule. Place the fork and knife in position and dishes will be cleared.

Signal #4 - Check, please. Signal #2 with a twist- pretend to write something in the air and mouth silently the word check.

Signal #5 - Cue from Host. If you're not sure how to eat something, copy your host. If you're unsure of how many courses to order, follow your host.

GAME CHALLENGE #6: Name the Signal.

1. You are finished eating your meal. You should:
   a. Raise your hand to let the waiter know.
   b. Yell to the waiter - "Done."
   c. Do nothing.
   d. Use the 4:20 pm rule.

2. You need a new drink. You should:
   a. Yell, "Waiter, I need a drink!"
   b. Do nothing and hope he comes soon.
   c. Raise your arm slightly to get the waiters attention.

Tackle the Obstacle

What do you do if you order a meal and when you receive it, it isn't what you expected? Maybe it didn't come the way you ordered it? You can either choose to say nothing and eat it even though you don't really like it, be rude about it, or learn how to send it back. The goal is to handle all situations with respect, kindness and understanding. Don't worry your parents will help you, but it's time for you to step up and learn how to handle tough situations.

Problem : You received your yummy pasta but realized it wasn't at all what you thought it would be. You are so hungry but you can't eat what they just served you-they didn't put the cheese on the side!

Solution : You can try apologizing to the waiter and explain that you must have made a mistake ordering. Usually any restaurant that cares about its customer will try to make things right-especially if you are polite.

Problem : Your ice cream came but you dropped it on the floor.

Solution : Apologize to the waiter and he might bring you a new dessert.

GAME CHALLENGE #7: Can you find the solution to the problem?

Problem : The waiter brings you a cold coke and you are really thirsty. Suddenly you knock over your drink.

Solution :

112

CHALLENGE FOODS

> **CERTAIN FOODS ARE ACCEPTABLE TO EAT WITH OUR FINGERS.**

Certain foods are more challenging to eat than others. Some foods are acceptable to eat with our fingers. How do we know what to do?

Top FINGER FOOD Plays:

Sandwiches: A plain sandwich can be picked up and eaten with your hands. If it's a really big open-faced sandwich dripping with sauces and mushy fillings you should use a fork and knife.

Chips, French fries, chicken nuggets, hamburgers: Most fast foods are intended to be eaten with your hands. Although if it's a really big burger with lots of toppings, you might want to reach for the fork and knife.

BBQ: Ribs, hot dogs, chicken wings, and more. A BBQ is usually pretty informal so it is fine to pick up these foods with your fingers. But please use a napkin and try to resist licking your yummy fingers!

> **TIME OUT!**
> Q: How do you fix a broken tomato?
> A: With tomato paste!

Cookies: No need for a fork and knife. Just watch the crumbs!

> French Fries are one of the most popular fast foods in the U.S.

Bacon: If the bacon is crispy, it's better to use your hands. If you try to cut the bacon it will probably only crumble.

Hors d'oeuvres & crudite: Party foods are intended to be eaten with your fingers.

Pizza: How do you like your pie? Pizza can be served and eaten in different ways. Here are the options:

1. Use a knife and fork to cut the pizza. This is the most polite way and works well if you have a lot of toppings.

2. Use your hands and fold the slice in half. Create a "U" in the crust to help hold the cheese and the toppings.
3. Use your hands without folding the pizza. This is the most preferred and easiest way to eat.

Corn on the Cob: Hold the corn firmly with two hands. Begin eating a few rows from left to right. Careful not to look like a typewriter going back and forth. And do not eat in a circle around the corn. Eat as neatly as you can without making unnecessary gnawing sounds. Take small bites and use the napkin.

Top DIFFICULT FOOD Plays:

Soup: Always spoon your soup away from you in the bowl. Why move if further from you when you are trying to bring it to your lips? Spooning

> EAT DIFFICULT FOODS AS CAREFULLY AS YOU CAN.

it away from you allows any soup that is going to dribble off to end up back In the bowl, instead of your shirt! Eat the soup from the side of your soup spoon. This prevents it from spilling off the spoon.

Cherry Tomatoes: Use the prong of your fork. Gently pierce the skin of the tomato to grab it and release some juices. If small, you can eat the tomato in one piece. If large, use a knife to cut it in half before eating. Be careful not to squirt your neighbor!

Hard Tacos: A nice crunchy taco should be picked up carefully. Wrap your hand around the back so that your hand blocks the filling. With the index and thumb GENTLY squeeze the taco shut. Take small bites from the side. Use your fork to help pick up the inside filling that spills out. If the taco crumbles apart, use your fork and knife and eat it like a taco salad.

Quesadillas: A very large quesadilla should be eaten with a knife and fork. Too much filling would fall out if you tried to eat it with your hands.

Spaghetti: Spaghetti can be eaten three different ways:

1. Use a fork and begin twirling a few strands onto the fork.

2. Use a fork and cut the pasta with the side of the fork.

3. Ask for a pasta spoon to help you twirl. Use a fork and begin twirling the pasta strands inside the spoon.

Peas: Peas should be eaten with a fork. Try to scoop them up into the fork with the help of the knife. Or pierce them gently with a fork.

Ice Cream: A delicious treat! Use a spoon if it comes in a bowl. Eat small bites. Although tempting, do not lick the bowl.

TIME OUT!
Q: When the chef was baking a cake, why did he run away?
A: Because the recipe said to crack 2 eggs and then beat it.

RULE BREAKERS!

✤ DON'T double dip in the sauce.

✤ DON"T mush up the ice cream and make soup. No licking the bowl.

✤ DON'T lick your fingers after using your hands to eat finger foods.

GAME CHALLENGE #8: True or False:

1. Sarah is allowed to eat her hamburger with her hands.

2. Joe should lick his fingers after eating a delicious taco.

3. Jay should use a knife and fork when eating a hard taco.

S M A R T

MANNERS @ THE RESTAURANT

Your behavior at a restaurant affects not only your family but everyone around you. Besides using all the basic mealtime manners, be aware of these restaurant specific manners.

> WE NEED TO USE OUR BEST MEALTIME MANNERS. AS OUR BEHAVIOR AFFECTS EVERYONE AROUND US.

Top RESTAURANT BEHAVIOR Plays:

✤ Wait to be seated in more formal restaurants.

✤ Stay at the table until the meal ends. Should you need to use the bathroom, please excuse yourself.

✤ Keep food on the plate or in your mouth, not on the table or floor.

✤ Keep your shoes on and your hands and feet to yourself.

✤ Use your indoor voice to not disturb others.

✤ Use your table manners. Ask your parents for help if you have trouble cutting.

✤ Relax and enjoy with your family-participate in dinner conversation.

> Why don't my parents bring me to a nice restaurant?

How to say "Bon Appétit" in different languages?
"Buon Appetito" - Italian
"Buen Provecho" - Spanish
"Guten Appetit" - German
"Velbekomme" - Danish
"Smakelijk" - Dutch
"Smaklig Maltid" - Swedish
"Afiyet Olsun" - Turkish

The Formal Setting Review

Many restaurants use a more formal table setting.
Here they add some additional players to a more basic
setting. You might have an extra glass and more forks and knives.
Remember the most important rule is start with the utensil on the outside
and work your way in. When in doubt watch your parents or friends!

Top FORMAL TABLE SETTING Plays:

+ Put your napkin on your lap.
+ Use the **outside-in rule.** Start with the small fork if you order a
   salad or appetizer and then move on to the big fork for the entrée.
+ Use the **spoon on the right** for your soup (if you have one).
+ Utensils on the top of the plate are for the dessert.
+ The **water glass** is above the knife and the wine glass is above the spoon.
+ Use the **bread plate** on your left. Eat bread one bite at a time.
+ Use your **utensil signals** - resting positions and finished!

RULE BREAKERS!

+ DON'T play with the condiments - salt, sugar, jelly packets etc. Other
   people will use them and they don't want your germs on the condiments!
+ DON'T run around a restaurant. It is rude and dangerous. First of all,
   you will be in the way and secondly you could get something hot or
   sharp dropped onto you.
+ DON'T play games, text or talk on the phone during dinner. (You'll read
   more about this in the technology game plan.)
+ DON'T play under the table.
+ DON'T shout, scream, cry or fight with siblings!
+ DON'T chew with your mouth open.

GAME CHALLENGE #9: True or False. Discuss your answers with your parents

    1. Keep your shoes on and feet to yourself at a restaurant?

    2. I can use my iPad at the table while I wait for my food to arrive. I am bored and it will help pass the time.

    3. It is fine to eat the bread while I wait for my food.

WINNING PLAY REVIEW

Game Plan #4 - Restaurant Behavior

1. Match your look with the place or situation.
2. Dress options: informal, casual, business casual, casual elegant and formal.
3. Adjust your manners according to the type of restaurant. Create your rating system.
4. Be respectful and courteous to everyone that works in the restaurant and the people around us.
5. The host's job is to greet you at the door and seat you at your table.
6. The waiter serves you throughout your meal.
7. Be respectful to everyone that works in the restaurant.
8. The menu organizes the food into different courses.
9. Learn the big foodie words to understand restaurant talk.
10. When ordering, be decisive, speak clearly and politely.
11. Use the signals to communicate with your waiter.
12. Handle any issues with respect, kindness and understanding to find a good solution.
13. Certain foods are acceptable to eat with your fingers.
14. Use your best mealtime manners as your behavior affects everyone around you.

LET'S PRACTICE!

GAME ON!

SECTION 1. You make the call!

Fill in DO or DON'T. Complete this section and earn 10 tickets!

1._____ Wear sweatpants and a dirty shirt to a restaurant that is rated as a casual restaurant.

2._____ Order three courses when you go out to eat with your friend's family. After all they are paying so you might as well get as much food as you can!

3._____ Demand that the waiter get you a drink. "I need a drink, now! Very thirsty today!"

4._____ Your family is early to a dinner reservation. You stand patiently and wait for the restaurant to finish setting up your table.

5._____ Use your fingers to help eat spaghetti-especially as the pasta hangs down from your fork.

6._____ Order your steak medium well if you would like it be mostly brown with just a hint of pink.

7._____ Play your video game at the table while you are eating your dinner. It's boring to just sit and eat.

8._____ Come up with stories to share at dinner. It's always fun to have a great dinner conversation.

9._____ Demand a new drink after your sister has just spilled your drink.

10._____ Hold your hand up high and waive to get your waiter's attention. Maybe a little whistle will also help catch his attention!

11._____ Use the small fork on the outside to eat your first course.

12._____ Begin eating the bread as you wait for your meal to arrive.

SECTION 2. Scrimmage!

Recruit family and friends to play these games.
Each game is worth one ticket. The more times you play, the more you earn.

Fancy Table.- Once a week set up the dining room for a fancy family dinner party. Pretend that you are eating at a casual elegant restaurant. Dress for the occasion. Use the formal place setting. Bon Appétit!

Dress Code Alert! Read the following dress code to someone in your family. Quickly, what type of restaurant can you visit? Why? Name one thing that would make the dress even better? This could be anything from jewelry, shoes, tie etc.

1. Jeans and a red t-shirt
2. Khaki pants and an old baseball shirt
3. A sundress and ripped sneakers
4. A collared shirt and nice shorts
5. A bathing suit and bare feet

Waiter, please. Assign one person in your family to be the waiter. Have the assigned person take your orders and serve the meals.

Role Play.
   ✣ Play a very difficult customer at a restaurant. What type of things could you do to be rude and difficult to the waiter. What was unacceptable and why?
   ✣ Play a very polite customer at a restaurant. How could you act to be extra polite.

SECTION 3. Can you make the free throw?
- Earn 5 tickets! ☺

1. If you ordered an appetizer, entree and a drink, in which order will you receive them?

2. You go to a formal restaurant and when you sit down you notice they have two forks. Which fork should you use?

3. You have a plate with a big steak. How should you cut the steak?

4. What does the word 'Au Gratin' mean?

5. What are some top polite manner plays at the restaurant?

6. You just dropped your fork under the table. What should you do?

7. Your waiter serves you chicken with a salad when you ordered chicken with french fries. What should you do?

8. What is the signal to tell the waiter that you are finished?

9. The phrase "Bon Appétit" means "Enjoy your meal." True or false?

SECTION 4. Restaurant Behavior Crossword Puzzle

- Earn 5 tickets! ☺

Across ▷

4. Use _____ to communicate with your waiter.

6. When you _____ be decisive, speak clearly and politely.

7. The person whose job is to greet you at the door and seat you at the table.

Down ↓

1. The person who serves you throughout your meal.

2. A _____ to organize the food options.

3. Handle situations with respect, kindness and understanding to find a good _____ .

5. This type of table setting can often be found at an expensive restaurant.

Words to Play: Order, Host, Waiter, Menu, Solution, Formal

SECTION 5. Restaurant Behavior Word Search

- Earn 5 tickets! ☺

```
S R Q M D Q C H Q T X T S O H
J D B Y O G J H W R S W P Z J
R E O W U K K A L K H O V T Z
N E A O E N I V F R L G Y V F
V D S W F T E Y Q A G F E J O
J O J P E R Q M M Q U R E U R
C C W R E T E R X P C Y Z U M
J S U P Q C O G D A O F G E A
X S Y A I F T H N M R W J I L
Z E M A N N E R S I O R O D W
O R Q I X P L V Z R F L L S F
Z D P X V Z I Y I Y O I J O Q
D Q O F C H O V N F L N W E U
Z H T S K P Q Y I H H W Z C T
S D O O F T L U C I F F I D H
```

DIFFICULT FOODS   DRESS CODE

FINGER FOODS   FORMAL

HOST   INFORMAL

MANNERS   MENU

RESPECT   WAITER

ANSWERS

Game Challenges:

#1) Answers will vary. Talk to your coach.

#2) 1. B, 2. C, 3. A

#3) 1. **** or *****, 2. * or **

#4) Pasta served in a white sauce made with cream, butter and cheese.

#5) Answers will vary. Talk to your coach (an adult).

#6) 1. D, 2. C

#7) Apologize to the waiter and he will bring you a new drink.

#8) 1. T, 2. F, 3. F

#9) 1. T, 2. Ask your parents. 3. T

Game On:

SECTION 1. You make the call!

Don't, 2. Don't, 3. Don't, 4. Do, 5. Don't, 6, Do, 7, Don't, 8. Do, 9. Don't, 10. Don't, 11. Do, 12. Do.

SECTION 2. Scrimmage

Answers will vary. Please discuss answers with your coach (an adult).

SECTION 3.

1. Drink, appetizer and entrée., 2. Use the outside-in rule, 3. Cut a few pieces at a time and eat. Repeat., 4. Browned and buttered bread crumbs with cheese., 5. Discuss with a grown up., 6. Kindly ask the waiter for a new fork., 7. Kindly ask the waiter to correct the order. 8. 4:20 pm rule, 9. True

SECTION 4. Crossword Puzzle

Across ☺⇨ 4. Signals   6. Order   7. Host

Down ⬇ 1. Waiter   2. Menu   3. Solution   5. Formal

SECTION 5. Word Search

```
S + + + + + + + + + + T S O H
+ D + + + + + + W + + + + + +
R + O + U + + A + + + + + + +
+ E + O + N I + + + L + + + F
+ D S + F T E + + A + + + + O
+ O + P E R + M M + + + + + R
+ C + R E + E R + + + + + + M
+ S + + + C O G + + + + + + A
+ S + + + F T + N + + + + + L
+ E M A N N E R S I + + + + +
+ R + I + + + + + + F + + + +
+ D + + + + + + + + + + + + +
+ + + + + + + + + + + + + + +
+ + + + + + + + + + + + + + +
S D O O F T L U C I F F I D +
```

(Over, Down, Direction)

DIFFICULTFOODS(14,15,W)

DRESSCODE(2,12,N)

FINGERFOODS(11,11,NW)

FORMAL(15,4,S)

HOST(15,1,W)

INFORMAL(4,11,NE)

MANNERS(3,10,E)

MENU(8,6,NW)

RESPECT(1,3,SE)

WAITER(9,2,SW)

TICKET TALLY SCORE BOARD

Ask an adult to place a check on a ticket after each game challenge or practice section. How many tickets were you able to collect?

SCORE BOARD

X · X · X

DECODE THE DRESS CODE

Match your look with the place or situation

INFORMAL - Come as you are!

Jeans, Shorts, Pants, Sweatpants, Skirt, Casual Dress, T-Shirt, Sweatshirt, Long Sleeve Shirt, Collared Shirt, Sweater, Polo Shirt, Athletic Uniform, Casual Shoes

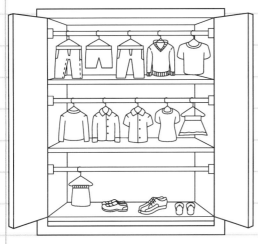

CASUAL - Comfortable yet presentable!

Jeans, Shorts, Pants, Skirt, Casual Dress, T-Shirt, Sweatshirt, Long Sleeve Shirt, Sweater, Collared Shirt, Polo shirt, Casual Shoes

CASUAL ELEGANT - Dress to impress!

Dress Pants, Dress Sweater, Party Dress or Skirt, Sweater Vest, Polo Shirt, Blazer, Dress Shirt, More Formal Shoes

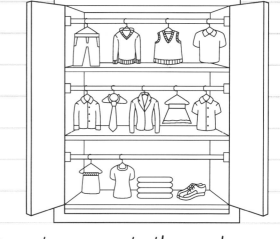

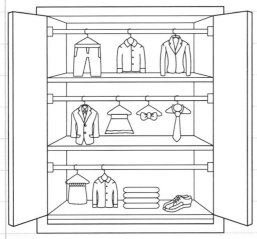

FORMAL - Dress to impress to the max!

Formal Pants & Shirts, Your Nicest Party Skirt or Dress, Blazer, Suit, Formal Shoes (When in doubt ask an adult for help!)

GAME PLAN #5 - TECHNOLOGY TALK

GOAL:
What happens when we combine the internet and etiquette?
You get NETIQUETTE - also known as technology and
manners. It's not complicated. Respect, politeness, safety
and making people feel comfortable apply to technology too.
Be a great digital citizen by showing good character online and
applying three technology rules:
- ☑ STAY SAFE & PRIVATE
- ☑ STAY RESPECTFUL
- ☑ STAY BALANCED IN LIFE

Life Skills Required:
- ✢ Basic Internet Safety
- ✢ Stop Cyberbullying!
- ✢ Digital Communication 101
- ✢ Strike a Balance

Equipment needed:
- ✢ You
- ✢ Parents, siblings and friends
  to practice

Game Directions:
- ✢ Take the challenges
- ✢ Have an adult check the box at the end of the game
  after you complete the challenge
- ✢ Cash in your tickets for the reward chosen with your coach (your parents)

Ticket Goal:_____

Game Prize:_____

BASIC INTERNET SAFETY

SAFETY

STAY SAFE & PRIVATE ONLINE.

As we travel the internet, we need to STAY SAFE & PRIVATE. Think of it as playing football. You wouldn't go out on the field without a helmet and with your eyes closed. You need to play with your eyes open and equipped with the proper safety equipment. Let's use the internet the same way - eyes open and with safety equipment.

TIME OUT!
Q: Why did the computer get sick?
A: He left his windows open!

Private Information

What is private and personal information? Anything that gives out important information about yourself is considered private and should not be shared. Your coach would never share a secret play with the competition, right?

- Name
- Parents' Names
- Height and weight
- Telephone number

- Where you live - city and address
- Birthdate
- Photo
- School

DETAILED INFORMATION ABOUT YOURSELF SHOULD NOT BE SHARED ON THE INTERNET.

VISIT PARENT- OR TEACHER- APPROVED WEBSITES ONLY. WHEN IN DOUBT ASK A GROWN UP.

Non-personal information such as your likes and dislikes can be shared on the internet. For example, you can share your favorite ice cream or song on the radio.

Safe Sites

What is a safe site? Your parents and teachers help you to determine which sites are educational, safe and fun! A site should never make you feel uncomfortable. It should be a site designed for kids and it should not ask for personal information. Safe sites often need your parent's permission to join. Again, if you stumble upon something that doesn't feel right, please tell a parent.

Password and Username Protection

As you visit sites, you will sometimes be asked to create a username and password. Both should not give out too much personal information about yourself. For example, you should not use your full name or the city where you live. The password should be kept private and only shared with your family. For safety reasons, change your password periodically so that no one can break the code. Here's your chance to be creative and come up with a unique player name. You can use colors, animals, music, sports and games-anything that won't reveal too much about yourself.

> **KEEP YOUR USERNAME AND PASSWORD PRIVATE AND SECURE.**

> **DO NOT OPEN UP EMAILS, POP-UPS, ATTACHMENTS FROM STRANGERS!**

> **GAME CHALLENGE #1:** What is the most safe password or username? Why?
> 1. Butterfliesjane
> 2. Butterflies
> 3. Janesmith
> 4. Jsmithbutterflies

Spam and Scams

Have you heard of the words SPAM and SCAMS? SPAM is any kind of unwanted online communication such as emails, instant pop up-messages, texts etc. A lot of computers are already set up with SPAM shields but sometimes a few might get through. Never open up any emails or attachments that you receive from people you don't know. Don't sign up for a "free newsletter" or check boxes that ask if you would like to receive updates. Some emails, pop-ups and attachments could be harmful to your computer. Also watch out for SCAMS! Scams are offers that target unsuspecting people, often to make a quick profit.

> **TIME OUT!**
> Q: How does a tree get into its computer?
> A: It has to LOG IN!

THINK AND ASK PERMISSION BEFORE SHARING PHOTOS. EMAILS & ATTACHMENTS.

Is Sharing Caring?

Think before you send! Any information shared on the internet is available to anyone. Always answer one question before sharing pictures, videos and attachments - "Is this something that my parents, teachers and grandparents would be fine sharing?" Again, once it's on the internet, it's out and very public. Even if you delete it later, you have no way of knowing if it was copied or forwarded. Family pictures should not be uploaded without prior permission from other family members or your parent's consent. And please do not open photos and attachments from strangers. Finally, never forward anyone else's emails, photos, attachments without their approval.

Keep Your Guard Up!

NEVER TALK TO STRANGERS ON THE INTERNET!

Faces are hidden on the internet. Any stranger can pretend to be a friend and you have no way of knowing who they are because they are behind the mask of the computer. The same rules that you know about strangers, apply to the internet. We don't open up doors for strangers. We never talk to strangers or follow them somewhere. Tell an adult if someone you don't know, a stranger, tries to talk to you online.

GAME CHALLENGE #3: Nicky has been talking to a boy named Joe online. Joe has told Nicky where he lives, how old he is and where he goes to school. Joe asks Nicky where he goes to school. What should Nicky do?

1. Tell Joe where he lives. After all Joe just shared with him so it would be rude not to reply.
2. Tell an adult and stop speaking with Joe.
3. Tell Joe that you cannot give out your personal information.

STOP CYBERBULLYING!

DO NOT PARTICPATE IN CYBERBULLYING AND REPORT INAPPOPRIATE BEHAVIOR.

What is a cyberbully? A cyberbully is a bully in the digital world. A cyberbully can spread rumors and lies. They sometimes post mean comments and use hurtful words. They tease and have very little sensitivity to the other person's feelings.

Cyberbullying is when someone bullies another person through the use of computers, cell phones and other devices. It can be done by one person or a group. Anyone can be a cyberbully. You don't need to be big and strong. Actions are very public, can be done at any time and be permanent. You may not like everyone you meet and not everyone will like you. That's normal. Maybe you are jealous about someone's look, athletic ability, how smart they are or a friendship. But there is no excuse for participating in cyberbullying.

CYBERBULLYING IS VERY PUBLIC AND IS PERMANENT!

Top CYBERBULLY PREVENTION Plays:

SHOW DIGITAL GOOD CHARACTER. BE YOURSELF. BE RESPECTUL & RESPONSIBLE. ASK PERMISSION.

⁜ Show Good Character
⁜ Be Yourself - Always be yourself online and tell the truth. Only post comments that you would say out loud in front of your parents or teachers.
⁜ Be Respectful - Send nice emails and texts. If you are angry take a time out to avoid sending an angry or threatening email or text.
⁜ Be Responsible - Tell a grown up if you see anyone acting like a cyberbully.
⁜ Have Tact - Choose to not participate in negative internet behavior.
⁜ Ask Permission - Send pictures and videos around only with your friends' and family's approvals.

RULE BREAKERS!

✣ DON'T harass, threaten, lie, embarrass or target anyone online.

✣ DON'T participate by doing nothing and watching someone be mean online.

✣ DON'T write something over the internet when you are angry or upset.

✣ DON'T share personal information online.

✣ DON'T share pictures of other people without their permission.

GAME CHALLENGE #4: List 5 ways to act to be a great digital citizen and have a positive technology experience!

1.

2.

3.

4.

5.

EXTRA CREDIT: Can you think of anything else?

DiGiTAL COMMUNiCATiON 101

Is digital communication more complicated than face-to-face? Yes, because without face-to-face communication, your identity, words or how you write can easily come across the wrong way. We need to be careful and remember that what we write shows who we are.

There are so many techy gadgets and we need to understand limits and continue to be courteous, kind and considerate while using technology.

> DIGITAL COMMUNICATION IS MORE DIFFICULT THAN FACE-TO-FACE COMMUNICATION.

Cell Phone Rules

The cell phone allows constant communication with everyone anytime. Imagine an athletic field where all the players were allowed to bring their coach and gadgets during the game. The interruption to the game would be tremendous! Simple cell phone rules for everyone can limit disruptive behavior.

Top CELL PHONE Plays:

❖ **Volume Control** - Lower your voice when talking in public. Use the silent ringer or silent mode in places such as a theater or a restaurant. Choose your ring tone wisely.

❖ **Pay Attention** - Talk on your cell phone when you are allowed to pay complete attention to the call. Avoid taking calls when you are in the middle of a face-to-face conversation. If you do have to take the call, ask permission of the person with you. For example, say "Excuse me. That's my mom. Would you mind if I take this?"

> BE CURTEOUS, KIND & CONSIDERATE TO OTHERS WHILE USING YOUR CELL PHONE.

✤ **Comfortable Space** - Use the 10-foot rule when talking on your cell phone. Stand about 10 feet away from the nearest person while talking on the phone. No one wants to listen to your conversation.

✤ **Sharing is Caring** - Be charitable with your phone. If you see a friend who can't seem to find his parents. Let them use your phone to call home.

RULE BREAKERS!

✤ DON'T light up a phone when in a dark theater.

✤ DON'T put your phone on speaker without the caller's permission.

✤ DON'T talk about personal topics when others can hear you. No one wants to know that you threw up this morning because you ate something gross!

✤ DON'T use a cell phone in the following places: bathroom, elevator, hospital, waiting room, auditorium, school, funeral, wedding, movie theater, bus, train, plane, library, museum, church or general place of worship

---

GAME CHALLENGE #5: Name top 3 cell phone good manner plays?

1.

2.

3.

Mind your Digital Manners!

TK- DO YOU WANT TO COME OVER :(Call me :)(XXOO ????
Say What? Sloppy communication skills can sometimes lead to misunderstandings. Understanding general email & texting rules can avoid confusion-especially since you're not having a face-to-face conversation!

> USE DIGITAL WRITING MANNERS TO AVOID MISUNDERSTANDINGS.

Top DIGITAL WRITING Plays:

❖ Write Back - Please respond to emails and texts whether it is an invitation, a hello etc. Just because someone doesn't ask for a response doesn't mean you should ignore them. We are all busy but a simple "thanks" or OK at least lets the sender know that you got it.

❖ Check It - It's easy to make a mistake when sending a quick email. Always proofread and use spell-check. Double check that you have the right email address/person. Use the subject heading for email. This will save your reader from wondering what the email is about. For example, if you have a homework question, just put "homework question" as the subject.

> TAKE A TIME OUT AND THINK BEFORE SENDING! DID YOU MIND YOUR MANNERS?

Write complete sentences. A complete sentence makes your email easier to read.

❖ Be Nice - To begin a text or email use a polite greeting or closing - "Hi" and then a "thank you" or an "I appreciate your help" or "Nice to hear from you" goes a long way. A nice email usually brings back a happy reply!

❖ Too Long? - Be short and to the point. For something long and important, you are better off picking up a phone. Try to write no more than five sentences for email.

- ❖ Watch Your Tech Language - Don't write in caps because it looks like you are SHOUTING! If you want to show that you are joking use a smiley icon :) to let the reader know you are having fun and not trying to be mean.
- ❖ Think Before Sending! If you think something might embarrass or offend someone, please don't send. You can't get it back once it sends. Also never forward an email on to others without asking the original sender for approval-it might be private.
- ❖ No Angry Typing! If you are angry and upset, please walk away from the computer and do not send something that you might regret later.
- ❖ No Junk Please! Please do not forward jokes, chain letters etc to everyone. Not everyone likes to receive these types of emails. Also if you attach something, it could have a virus that you send to someone. On the same note, be careful opening attachments and emails from strangers! Better to delete if you think it's junk.

RULE BREAKERS!

- ❖ DON'T write something sad or urgent that should be done over the phone or in person.
- ❖ DON'T write too quick - you might have typos and send to the wrong person.
- ❖ DON'T write bad words or embarrassing messages to friends. It can get you and your friend in trouble. What if a parent sees it while the phone is on a table?
- ❖ DON'T text in public places such as at the movies, a play, in a restaurant, during dinner etc.
- ❖ DON'T write something you would not say to someone in person or out loud.

GAME CHALLENGE #6: Write an email to a friend. Use your digital manners.

DECODING TECHY TALK

What does this message mean? TY for visiting. L8R. :()

Introducing a new language called TechyTalk-made up of shortened words and emoticons. To get started, use the chart below. Good luck decoding!

AVOID MISUNDERSTANDINGS. LEARN TO DECODE TECHY TALK.

TEXT	MEANING
TY	Thank you
IMHO	In my humble opinion
TTYL	Talk to you later
IDK	I don't know
BTW	By the way
LOL	Laugh out loud
CYA	See ya
BRB	Be right back
J/K	Just kidding
OIC	Oh I see
L8R	Later
BFF	Best Friends Forever
ILY	I love you
B/C	Because

EMOTICON	SYMBOLS:
:)	Happy
>:-(	Angry
:( )	Can't stop talking
:-9	Delicious
:(	Sad
^5	High Five
(()):**	Hugs and Kisses
:-o	Mouth Open Surprised!
:o	Shocked
@_@	Tired, trying to stay awake
:-@	Yelling

Fun & Game Gadgets

You might love to rock out but keep in mind that there are wrong and right places to do so. Please put away the gadgets at places where you should be paying attention. For example, if you are at your brother's basketball game, don't just sit and listen to music or play games. Pay attention to what's on the court in front of you!

TIME OUT!
Knock, Knock!
-Who's there?
Radio
-Radio who?
Radio not, here I come!

Top FUN & GAME GADGET Plays:

❖ **Volume Control** - Limit the noise volume in public places. If you are on a train listening to music make sure that the noise level is not too loud. Not everyone around you wants to hear your music. Playing a loud video game can also be distracting to others around you.

❖ **Bud Control** - Ear buds in your ear and your head down tells people "go away." So be mindful when you use them so that you don't discourage socializing with other friends.

❖ **Pause** - Always pause the game or music when others would like to talk to you or if someone new walks into the room and you need to greet them. Pull both ear buds out when someone is talking to you. Leaving one ear bud in says that you are not interested and really only half listening to what they are telling you. Leaving both in while they are talking is just plain disrespectful.

> USE NOISE CONTROL AND
> PAUSING WHEN USING
> ENTERTAINMENT GADGETS.

GAME CHALLENGE #7: What should you do?

You run into your friend while listening to your iPod. What should you do?

   1. Remove the ear buds to talk to your friend.

   2. Give a quick nod and continue to listen to your music.

   3. Remove one ear bud and talk to your friend while enjoying the music.

RULE BREAKERS!

❖ DON'T talk to someone with music playing loudly on your headphones.

❖ DON'T ignore someone while playing with electronic gadgets.

TIME OUT!
Q: Why did the musician put his laptop in the oven?
A: He wanted to burn his own CD.

BALANCE YOUR TIME

Technology is a lot of fun but make an effort to balance your time. Don't forget to read books, go outside, use your imagination and enjoy real sports and nature!

LIMIT TECHNOLOGY AND BALANCE YOUR LIFE WITH OTHER ACTIVITIES.

GAME CHALLENGE #8: Use your imagination! Doodle your favorite outside sport or activity.

WINNING PLAY REVIEW

Game Plan #5 - Technology Talk

1. Stay safe and private online.
2. Detailed information about yourself should not be shared on the internet.
3. Visit parent- or teacher-approved websites only. When in doubt, ask a grown up.
4. Keep your username and password private and secure.
5. Do not open up emails, pop-ups, or attachments from strangers.
6. Think and ask permission before sharing photos, emails and attachments.
7. Never talk to a stranger on the internet.
8. Do not participate in cyberbullying and report inappopriate behavior.
9. Cyberbullying is very public and permanent.
10. Show digital good character- Be yourself. Be respectful & responsible. Ask permission.
11. Technology communication is more difficult than face-to-face communication.
12. Be courteous and considerate to others while using your cell phone.
13. Use digital writing manners to avoid misunderstandings.
14. Take a time out and think before sending! Did you mind your manners?
15. Avoid misunderstandings by learning how to decode techy talk.
16. Practice noise control and pausing when using entertainment gadgets.
17. Limit technology and balance your life with other activities.

LET'S PRACTICE!

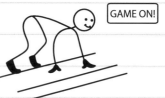

GAME ON!

SECTION 1. You make the call!

Fill in DO or DON'T. Complete this section and earn 10 tickets!

1. _____ Cindy emails, "I'm having a party and you are not invited."
2. _____ Cindy emails, "I like your new haircut."
3. _____ Cindy texts, "Thanks for the advice."
4. _____ Cindy texts, "Did you finish your homework?"
5. _____ Cindy texts, "You are such a freak!"
6. _____ Cindy texts, "I DON"T WANT TO COME OVER TODAY."
7. _____ Cindy texts, "You are STUPID."
8. _____ Cindy gives out your secret codes and passwords to your friends.
9. _____ Cindy opens up an email or instant message from a stranger.
10. _____ Cindy opens up an email with an attachment from a friend.
11. _____ Jen is talking to her friend online when she gets a message saying there is trouble with her computer and she needs to type in her online password again. She types it in.
12. _____ Cindy shares her favorite song with a stranger online.
13. _____ Cindy shares her favorite teacher with a stranger online.

SECTION 2. Can you make the free throw? - Earn 10 tickets! ☺

1. If someone sends me an inappropriate message or material, I should:
   a. Never reply to these messages and tell a grown up.
   b. Tell all my friends.
   c. Keep it secret.
   d. Reply to the message and ask the sender to stop sending me messages.

2. If someone I meet online asks me to keep a secret from a parent, I should:
   a. Keep the secret.
   b. Tell my parents because no one should ask me to keep a secret from my parents.
   c. Tell all my friends.

3. When you are making up a username for email and instant messaging, you should:
   a. Always use your real name.
   b. Use a name that doesn't reveal your true identity.
   c. Use a name that gives good clues about who you really are.

4. With your secret codes and passwords, you should:
   a. Give them out to your best friends.
   b. Give them out to anyone that asks.
   c. Never give out your passwords, except to your parents.

5. What information is okay to give out on the internet?
   a. Last name
   b. School name
   c. Favorite TV show
   d. My address

6. You are talking to someone online, and they know some of the same people you know. Since they have many of the same friends as you, is it okay to give them your phone number if they ask?
   A. Yes
   B. No

7. If someone online tells you they are in the eighth grade, they are probably how old?
   a. 15
   b. 12
   c. 13
   d. There's no way to tell.

8. You can send someone a picture of yourself over the internet when:
   a. It is for a school assignment only.
   b. You have a friend with you in the room.
   c. Your parents approve.
   d. You are applying for a modeling job.

SECTION 3. Scrimmage!

Recruit family and friends to play these games.
Each game is worth one ticket. The more times you play, the more you earn.

NO TECHNOLOGY HERE! - At a family gathering create a basket where all the guests and family members have to leave their electronics in the basket.

DECODING - Can you break the code? Take turns and use the tech language guide to test your partner's knowledge on techy talk and emoticons. For example, what does this mean : () ?

CYBERBULLY PREVENTION - Role Play. You are introducing a first timer to the internet, please tell her the most important cyberbully prevention plays online.

ONLINE CYBERBULLY CASE - John checked his texts. He had just written a joke about pigs and emailed the joke to five friends. Most of his friends responded with a LOL (laugh out loud) or a smiley face. But the last comment sent to the whole group said, "John is an ugly pig!"
  - How might John have felt after the comment posted?
  - If you were John's friend and you saw his post, what would you say?
  - Should John reply to all with another mean comment back?
  - What should he do?

DIGITAL WRITING - Role Play. Your friend just received her first iPod and is excited to start texting others. Please give her the top five digital communication plays.

SECTION 4. Technology Talk Crossword Puzzle

- Earn 5 tickets! ☺

Across ▷

2. We need to show good _____ on-line.

3. How we write and speak.

6. Important information about yourself.

7. Acting in a way that shows you care about their feelings and well-being. We need to stay _____ online.

Down ▽

1. A word used to describe internet and etiquette.

2. A bully in the digital world.

4. Learn to have _____ in your life.

5. Learn the _____ sites to play on the internet. Remember eyes open and use the right equipment.

6. The internet is a very _____ place. Emails, photos and comments can be seen by anyone and is permanent.

Words to Play: Cyberbully, Character, Private, Netiquette, Balance, Language, Public, Safe, Respectful

SECTION 5. Technology Talk Word Search – Earn 5 tickets! ☺

```
I N T E R N E T S A F E T Y M
I T V Z E E N C X J S L B C N
C V B F V L S G A A M N C E T
Y G O B D N C P F T O D Z Y C
B L A E R Z N E O U Q I X M E
E V C Z C Q S E W N T K D D P
R Y O P E I S A T I S D A B S
B S F I T V M V C A C I S W E
U O D E C N A L A B V L B L R
L C S S S P A M S T I I S L A
L I C K P T Z J F A E R R K E
Y F O J I N S Q M H I X T P R
F T F G I M T E B I Z R T D R
J T I Q M H X J U F A S Z S D
A D P X W Q S A I C C W F I U
```

BALANCED	CYBERBULLY
DIGITAL CITIZEN	EMAILS
INTERNET SAFETY	PRIVATE
RESPECT	RESPONSIBLE
SAFE SITES	SPAMS
TEXTS	

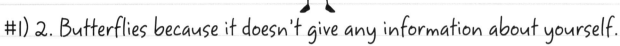

ANSWERS

Game Challenges:

#1) 2. Butterflies because it doesn't give any information about yourself.

#2) 1.This information shows your location. 2. Yes, 3. Yes, 4. Yes, 5. No. Careful-this can also show where you live.

#3) 2

#4) Answers may vary. Please discuss with your coach (an adult).

#5) Answers may vary. Please discuss with your coach (an adult).

#6) Answers may vary. Please discuss with your coach (an adult).

#7) 1

Game On:

SECTION 1. You make the call!

1. Don't, 2. Do, 3. Do, 4. Do, 5. Don't, 6. Don't, 7. Don't, 8. Don't, 9. Don't, 10. Do* Be careful! 11. Don't, 12. Don't- Be careful. Do not talk to strangers!, 13. Don't.

SECTION 2.

1. A, 2. B, 3. B, 4. C, 5. C, 6. B, 7. D, 8. C

SECTION 3. Scrimmage

Answers may vary. Please discuss with your coach (an adult).

SECTION 4. Crossword Puzzle

Across ☺⟹ 2. Character   3. Language   6. Private   7. Respectful

Down ⬇ 1. Netiquette   2. Cyberbully   4. Balance

SECTION 5. Word Search

```
I  N  T  E  R  N  E  T  S  A  F  E  T  Y  +
+  +  +  +  +  E  +  +  +  +  S  +  +  +  N
C  +  +  +  +  S  +  +  A  +  +  +  E  T
Y  +  +  +  +  +  P  F  +  +  +  Z  +  C
B  +  +  +  +  +  E  O  +  +  I  +  +  E
E  +  +  +  +  S  E  +  N  T  +  +  +  P
R  +  +  +  I  +  +  T  I  S  +  +  +  S
B  +  +  T  +  +  +  C  A  +  I  S  +  E
U  +  D  E  C  N  A  L  A  B  V  L  B  +  R
L  +  S  +  S  P  A  M  S  T  I  I  +  L  +
L  +  +  +  T  +  +  +  A  E  +  R  +  E
Y  +  +  +  I  +  +  +  M  +  +  X  +  P  +
+  +  +  G  +  +  +  E  +  +  +  +  T  +  +
+  +  I  +  +  +  +  +  +  +  +  +  S  +
+  D  +  +  +  +  +  +  +  +  +  +  +  +
```

(Over, Down, Direction)

CYBERBULLY(1,3,S)

DIGITALCITIZEN(2,15,NE)

EMAILS(8,13,NE)

INTERNETSAFETY(1,1,E)

PRIVATE(14,12,NW)

RESPECT(15,9,N)

RESPONSIBLE(5,1,SE)

SAFESITES(11,2,SW)

SPAMS(5,10,E)

TEXTS(10,10,SE)

TICKET TALLY SCORE BOARD

Ask an adult to place a check on a ticket after each game challenge or practice section. How many tickets were you able to collect?

SCORE BOARD
X · X · X

Notes:

SMART

TECH CODE OF CONDUCT

I promise to use all technology responsibly. This includes cell phone, computer, tablet, Xbox, Wii, iPods and any website that I visit or join. Please check the following statements to show that you have read them and understand them:

- ☐ I will not give away personal information such as my address, phone number, school information without my parent's consent.
- ☐ I will not befriend people that I have not met in real life without my parent's consent.
- ☐ I will never say anything unkind toward anyone for any reason on the internet.
- ☐ If I see someone being mean to another person, I will tell them to stop and then tell my parents.
- ☐ If someone is mean to me online I will not respond. I will instead tell my parents.
- ☐ I am not allowed to lie about my age to join any website or to use an app.
- ☐ I will stay courteous, respectful and considerate while using all technology.
- ☐ I will never forward any photos or information written by someone else without their permission.
- ☐ I will never share photos where I am posing in a way that I wouldn't in front of my parents.
- ☐ I will not download music, games or software without my parent's consent.
- ☐ I will never use inappropriate language online.
- ☐ I will immediately close any pop-up boxes with the x button.
- ☐ I understand that people are not always who they say they are, not everyone tells the truth and there is no such thing as privacy online.
- ☐ I will not sign up for anything online without my parent's consent
- ☐ I will always tell my parents if something makes me uncomfortable on the internet - an email, a website etc.
- ☐ I will take care of all my technology gadgets and remember that they are expensive.

_____   _____
     Player Signature   Coach Signature

THESMART♟PLAYBOOK™

CERTIFICATE OF SMART ACHIEVEMENT

S M A R T

AWARDED TO:

CONGRATULATIONS ON PLAYING IT SMART!

SIGNATURE

DATE

THESMART PLAYBOOK™

Made in the USA
San Bernardino, CA
28 September 2014